I LUVZ MONEY

Resolving your Love/Hate relationship with money

Learn more and follow the story at

www.ILuvzMoney.com

Look for more books by Matthew Randall at

www.MattRandall.com

Copyright © 2019 by Matthew Randall

All right reserved. No part of this book may be reproduced, scanned, or distributed in any printed, digital, or electronic format without permission.

Printed in the United States of America

Back cover headshot photo by 'Raya on Assignment'.

DEDICATION

This book is dedicated to all those amazing mentors I have had over the decades who tried their darnedest to help me achieve my dreams. Sorry it took me so long, but I think the student is finally ready.

For my family, who puts up with my eccentricities and somehow is always willing to follow me through these crazy adventures. Ok, so you laugh all the way and follow just for the humor, but thanks for not having me committed to an asylum.

For my parents, who I reference quite often throughout the book, and who always kept their skeletons carefully hidden in the closet. May they forgive me for 'airing their dirty laundry' in public.

For the many friends who encouraged me to write this and provided positive feedback along the way. I am ever so grateful for your support and faith through this process.

DISCLAIMER

There ain't no free lunch.

You get what you give.

This book doesn't work unless you do.

This can be 'self-help' or shelf-help'. The choice is yours.

If this book helps you become rich, reach back and help someone else.

This publication contains the opinions and ideas of this author. It is intended to provide helpful and informative material on the subjects addressed in the publication. It is sold with the understanding that the author is not engaged in rendering financial advice, is not a professional financial advisor, and does not provide specific financial advice. The reader should consult with a qualified financial advisor before adopting any of the suggestions in this book or inferences from it. The author and publisher specifically disclaim all responsibility for any liability, loss, or risk, personal or otherwise, that is incurred as a consequence, directly or indirectly, of the use and application of any of the contents of this book.

A PROMISE TO YOU

I can't promise you will become rich by reading this book. Nobody can. But, I can promise that I will keep the chapters short and the writing easy to read. I will be direct with real-life nuts-and-bolts information as much as possible. I will make the exercises relevant and encourage action, not just a bunch of make-you-feel-good motivation. I can promise you that there will be moments of humor and moments of slap-you-in-the-face reality.

This book is designed with exercises at the end of almost every chapter and space to write some notes or ideas. They are meant to be simple, yet thought-provoking. Please take advantage of the opportunity to brainstorm and get creative.

TABLE OF CONTENTS

PROLOGUE 1
   LOVE, HATE, AND MONEY 2
   TRUE CONFESSIONS 5
PART ONE WHAT IS MONEY? 11
   WHAT IS MONEY? 12
   CAN YOU REALLY LUVZ MONEY? 18
   WHY IS IT SO HARD TO TALK ABOUT MONEY? 22
   WHAT DOES IT MEAN TO BE RICH? 29
   WHY DO YOU WANT TO BE RICH? 33
   Part One Summary 37
PART TWO THE MONEY MINDSET 38
   OPPORTUNITIES ARE ENDLESS, OR ARE THEY? 39
   IT'S ALL IN YOUR HEAD 47
   ABUNDANCE VS LACK 52
   GOOD LUCK AND BAD LUCK 61
   THINK BIG. NO, BIGGER! 64
   YOUR WHY MUST BE BIGGER THAN YOUR BUT 67
   WHY POSITIVE AFFIRMATIONS DON'T WORK 72
   DON'T KEEP UP WITH THE JONES', CONGRATULATE THEM 76
   THIS IS ALL A BUNCH OF CRAP! 82
   Part Two Summary 87
PART THREE WHAT'S THE PLAN? 88
   HOW WILL YOU GET RICH? 89
   MATT'S DEFINITION OF RICH 91
   THE TWO ROADS TO RICHES 95
   THE 70-10-10-10 RULE 104
   CONSISTENCY IS THE 80% PROBLEM AND SOLUTION 109
   YOUR PERSONAL MIRACLE MORNING 113
   USING THE 5 W'S TO MAKE SMART MONEY DECISIONS 117
   Part Three Summary 121
PART FOUR YOUR LEGACY 122
   WHAT WILL YOU LEAVE BEHIND? 123
EPILOGUE 130
   WHAT ARE YOU READING? 131
   SUGGESTED READING LIST 135
ABOUT THE AUTHOR 138

PROLOGUE

/ˈprōˌlôg/

noun: **prologue**; plural noun: **prologues**

1. a separate introductory section of a literary or musical work.
   "this idea is outlined in the prologue"

2. an event or action that leads to another event or situation.
   "civil unrest in a few isolated villages became the **prologue to** widespread rebellion"

LOVE, HATE, AND MONEY

"Money is not the most important thing in the world. Love is. Fortunately, I love money."

~ *Jackie Mason, American actor and comedian*

What is this Love/Hate relationship nonsense all about? Of course, I love money. Why would anyone hate money? That's just crazy talk.

I humbly suggest that if you are not as rich as you want to be, then you have a relationship with money that is pushing it away from you like a bad marriage. I would know. I was there also for about 50 years until I discovered the secrets begin shared in this book. No, not exactly correct. Let's rephrase that...until I learned to believe in, accept, and actually apply the secrets being shared in this book.

Like too many others, possibly even you, I read a whole bunch of classic motivational books about life and money over the years, then carefully put them back on the shelf and went back to doing what was in my comfort zone, never making any real changes. As a matter of course, I did what I always did and got what I always got, and couldn't understand why I felt like the proverbial hamster on a wheel. I'm hoping by sharing my story that you will take these lessons to heart and begin to make a shift that will lead you to the riches you want, and so truly deserve. I did and it made all the difference.

So, what do I mean by 'resolving your love/hate relationship with money'? First, look at the word 'resolving'. To resolve is to settle a situation or to make a decision on a course of action. What it will take for you to improve your economic situation and become rich is some personal resolve and focus. I'm making a huge assumption here that because you picked up this book, you have an interest in money, making more of it, and becoming rich, because if you are going to have money, why not have a bunch of it? Second, 'relationship'. Let's look at money as your partner in life and business. The reality is that you and money cannot survive without each other. It's time we began to look at money as not some evil thing we have to use to get what we want, but rather a trusted friend we will take a fantastic journey with. Last, 'love/hate'. In order for us to have more money, we need to stop pushing it away. "But, but, but..." According to the Law of Attraction, which I'm sure you have heard of, if money is not being attracted to you in increasing quantities, then you are, by logic and reason, existing with one of two mindsets; you have enough and that's enough, or you don't deserve to have more. This is what I describe as pushing money away.

Learning to love money is not easy, especially when so many friends, relatives, and even people you admire will tell you that living money is evil. They will inadvertently hold you back from achieving your dreams because who you are becoming will be too far outside their comfort zone. For you to even say aloud in public, "I Luvz Money!" is considered rude, crude, and socially unacceptable. For you to shout it from the rooftops would be cause to have you restrained and sent for psychiatric evaluation. Yet, I'm going to tell you that this is exactly what you need to become a money magnet. When you are able to speak freely, openly, and confidently, about money with anyone, anywhere, then you can stop pushing it away and attracting more of it. You will also attract others who will support you on this journey. You may also lose a few acquaintances along the way who are not able to keep up.

You will learn more about my family issues surrounding money throughout this book, but now I can tell you that I associate with many people who are highly successful in their businesses and make tons of money. Some are millionaires and some are CEO's of major corporations. Guess what they talk about at parties and other social gatherings??? Yup, money. Wealthy individuals have no problem sharing how much they purchased their new home or boat for, how much they sold their business for, how much they invested in new equipment, how much their stock value is worth, when they plan to expand, where they will go on vacation, how much college tuition is for their kids, and any other topic around money. In fact, if you are not prepared to share at that level, then they are very disappointed in the conversation. I'm not saying that you need to perform at their level, just be able to share openly. The number of zeros in the conversation is irrelevant.

If you think that having a conversation about your's or someone else's new purchase of a ski lodge in Aspen, is inappropriate or bragging, then you are missing a huge point. It's not bragging unless it is intended to be. It's simply what rich people do and what they talk about because they have resolved their love/hate relationship with money. They get it, and because they get it, they have more of it. You can be there also, at the party, having open and meaningful conversations about your investments, homes, cars, trips, business interests, and so much more. I can tell you it's a whole lot more fun than sitting around the dining table complaining about the transmission starting to fail on your old junker and wondering how you will get to work so you don't get fired.

Are you ready to take this journey with me?

Come on, let's get rich together and learn to Luvz Money!

TRUE CONFESSIONS

This is the book that took me just one month to write, but includes 50+ years of experience and 10 years of agonizing over how to write it. I hope you not only enjoy reading it, but put it into action and get rich much sooner than I did.

Let's start with a true confession - I don't have a tear-jerking rags-to-riches story like so many other writers. This is not a story about how I was a poor kid from a broken home and suddenly discovered the key to wealth and happiness. Many other writers have endured far worse than I in their lives and have become far more successful than I. Anthony Robbins will tell you that he had a glandular issue that caused him to grow freakishly tall and his mom had a string of boyfriends/husbands who were abusive. Dr. Wayne Dyer will tell you a great story about his childhood struggling with attention issues and teachers who thought he wouldn't make it. Even Albert Einstein was told that because of his learning challenges in school, he wouldn't become successful. The list could go on all day and I would highly recommend you read their stories. They are amazing individuals to have done so well coming from backgrounds where most have simply given up trying.

I discovered later in life, like around 50, that my real problem has always been that I didn't have a childhood full of difficulty and struggle. I was a victim of what I now consider the 'Middle-class Curse' (MCC). What I mean by that is I grew up to believe that good enough was good enough. Yes, there was always the dream of making it rich and famous some day, but the truth about MCC is that no matter what you say outwardly, it leads you to believe deep down in your soul that as long as the bills are paid, life is pretty good. This is truly a curse that causes you to remain well-fed and totally unremarkable. The same was not true for my parents in their early years, however.

My mother was born in July of 1926 in the southeast corner of Prussia which is now part of Poland. In 1939, my mother was just 13 when Hitler invaded Poland. Her father was employed by the railroad, which meant three things; being Catholic, not Jewish, he was allowed to keep his job; they made just enough money to be lower middle-class; and he had access to advanced information from the government. Food was rationed and all good citizens needed to do their part to support the country. My mother recalled times being very tight and tensions high. If they could not finish their meal, it was wrapped and placed on top of the cabinets for when they got hungry again. Chocolate was a very rare treat for the kids, and they raised a pig in the backyard, illegally, for additional food. Being caught with an illegal pig could have cost them everything. When her father got a message that the Russian troops were advancing through their area, my mother was sent across two countries, by herself, to find her brother in Berlin. That is another story for another time, but she did make it as a young teen traveling unescorted, 800km+ by rail and boat.

Why am I telling you this story? Being born just after WWI and living as a teen through WWII, followed by the times of tough rebuilding after losing/surviving two wars, my mother's perception of money was forever engraved on her brain. Some of her favorite sayings were "Money is the root of all evil", "Money changes people", "Rich people are crazy", and more. These views were, of course, handed down to her children, me and my brother. We were raised to be frugal (another of my mother's favorite words), to save everything and never to be wasteful. In fact, being wasteful in our home was actually considered a sin. Mondays were always leftover nights and "a penny saved was a penny earned". She would drive us across town to save 2 cents on a gallon of gas.

Now, my father was born in 1930 in Dover, NH, USA. His parents married and opened a pharmacy in 1926. If you recall, October of 1929 was the big stock market crash that threw our country and the world into financial chaos. Things were good in the few years leading to the Great Depression, but afterwards they were very tough. People still needed their medications. My grandfather forgave many debts and as my grandmother would say, "He would have given away the store if I hadn't put my foot down". My father recalls an area of Dover, which is now subsidized public housing, that was littered with tents in the 1930s and they called it 'Shanty Town'. For those who couldn't afford apartments or homes, this is where they raised their families and some of them were my father's friends in school. My grandparents donated plenty of hand-me-down clothing to children from that neighborhood.

My father joined the army during the Korean War era, was stationed in Germany where he met my mother, and they moved back to the US when his tour was over in 1955. My father went to work as a pharmacist with his father and eventually took over the business around 1970 where he did OK, but we were certainly told we weren't rich. We had an old farm home that my parents bought from his cousin in 1970 for a song. It was in such need of updating that there was still a hand pump in the kitchen for water. I remember watching the walls being torn down as we had it gutted and seeing the mice run up and down the studs. As a five year old, I couldn't imagine living in this dump, but they turned it into a nice home and I finally had my own room. Throughout childhood, my weekends were filled with fun and exciting things to do like, mowing the lawn, gardening, home repairs, painting, chopping and stacking wood for the stoves, vacuuming the pool, and so many other wonderful experiences. Today I am grateful for the lessons, but not so much when I was in elementary school.

Being in a family business, I would hear phrases such as, "Money doesn't grow on trees", "Everything has a cost", "I have to work hard to pay for these things", "I can't just give things away, they are expensive". My personal favorite was, "It's always better to repair it, than replace it", which we spent many hours doing with all of our yard equipment and home appliances. My father was the king of finding creative ways to resurrect dead equipment.

Having explained how difficult it was for my parents as children, I was born at the end of the baby-boomer era when the economy was growing. Business improved for my parents and we were able to afford some luxuries. My grandmother helped us with some funds to install a pool. I was able to attend summer camps and eventually my parents paid college tuition for me and my brother. We did OK and I never had to starve or sell all my toys to get by. Yes, there were times when business was rough, but my parents never talked about it or let us know how bad things were. We did wonder why my father was losing his hair in clumps, but it somehow came back when business improved. Thank God, because the toupee looked terrible. (LOL)

Without realizing it, as all parents do, what they handed down to me, for better or for worse, was a philosophy about money that comes in many parts:

Money is something you have to work hard for.

Don't trust banks.

Be happy with what you have.

Being too rich is a curse.

Rich people do stupid things with their money.

You are rich when you have good friends and family.

I, fortunately or not, inherited the entrepreneurial bug. I was not interested in carrying on with the family pharmacy, but I did start my first business at 17 while in high school. Maybe some other time, we can talk about that. In college, at the age of 20, I earned my black belt in TaeKwonDo and knew what I wanted to do for a living. I would open a martial academy and become rich. At the same time, a friend of mine had a small club on the University of New Hampshire campus, where I attended, and he wanted to move to Florida. So, I adopted his students and opened my second business while a junior in college where I taught martial arts four nights a week. This turned into the next 30+ years of full-time martial arts school ownership, where, in the height of my business, we were the largest school in the state.

Like my parents and their parents, my business did pretty well in the good times and had some difficult years also. I made enough money, but never to the point where I would remotely be considered rich. It took me 50 years to figure out that my lack of over-the-top success in business was the result of two things: my parent's hand-me-down attitudes towards money that didn't serve me well, and my lack of consistent focus as a result of my ADD. Both of these will be addressed here in this book with the fondest desire that you can relate and it helps you to become as rich as you desire to be.

If you are ready to start your journey on the road to riches, then say "I Luvz Money!".

If you are really ready, then get up, stand tall, click your heels three times and repeat "I Luvz Money!" out loud until you can picture yourself with pockets overflowing.

Hey, Dorothy, if you can't have fun, then it's not worth it.

PART ONE
WHAT IS MONEY?

"I once thought of money as some evil thing that we all needed to have and struggle for, but if we had too much, then it would corrupt us. Now, I understand that money is simply a tool, no different from a hammer. It won't change who you are inside, but it does have the power to help good people do even more good for their family, friends, and communities. Money helps people live richer, more exciting, and more fulfilling lives. The more money you have, the more good you can do, for yourself and others."

~ Matthew Randall

WHAT IS MONEY?

"WHATEVER may be said in praise of poverty, the fact remains that it is not possible to live a really complete or successful life unless one is rich. No man can rise to his greatest possible height in talent or soul development unless he has plenty of money; for to unfold the soul and to develop talent he must have many things to use, and he cannot have these things unless he has money to buy them with."

~ Wallace D. Wattles, 'The Science of Getting Rich'

According to dictionary.com - "money", noun, "money is a current medium of exchange in the form of coins and banknotes; coins and banknotes collectively."

I don't know about you, but this definition means absolutely nothing to me. By definition, money is nothing but paper that we have assigned a certain value to. It is a placeholder for goods and services that people exchange. Nothing more. Nothing less. Yet, we attach so much mystery, value, and meaning to it when it's really just a representation of what a government decides it's worth through a very complicated and incomprehensible system of calculations and predictions.

On a side note, I had the pleasure of meeting the president of Crane Currency a few years ago where he explained how they make the 'paper' that our money is printed on. Turns out that it's not paper at all. It's mostly chewed up old denim jeans. Most of our 'paper cash' is actually cotton. That's how it can survive the laundry machine. Just thought you might find that interesting. Oh, and launder your money now and then. It's covered in germs. I mean in the machine, not the illegal way, of course.

Back on track (remember that ADD thing?), aside from printed cotton, what is this thing we call money? Before money was created, there was the barter system. This is where goods and services are traded for an agreed-upon value of other goods and services. If I needed warm animal pelts to survive the winter and you needed vegetables from my garden, we would agree on how much of each was a fair exchange. When it became burdensome to carry around pelts and vegetables everywhere, someone very wise decided to create metal coins and assign them a value presumably based on how much gold and silver was stored in some castle that could back up the value of those coins. This was a great idea because you could now buy whatever you needed from almost anyone without finding a direct trade.

The barter system is still alive and well, however, in many parts of the world today. In fact, in 1998 when our second son was born, we were amazed to find that our local doctor was still accepting chickens and eggs in exchange for his medical services. No, we didn't live in the backwoods of the Amazon. This was in Maine. We didn't have any chickens, so we needed to pay with our insurance plan, but it was pretty cool to see people bring in a basket of eggs for their checkup.

After the invention of coins for currency, banks were established, and then the invention of the banknote, which I believe to be the precursor to paper money, but honestly it's been a long time since my economics classes in college and someone smarter than me might have a better explanation, but it works for us right now. This brings us up-to-date with the Federal Reserve, right? Forget it. I'm not going to try to explain that one. That's a can of worms and a sore subject for many.

So, money is simply a representation of what the government, combined with the banks, and other shadow organizations, feels is a fair value for use in purchasing goods and services. That's all. Nothing more. Then, why do we give it so much attention and personal value? Simply put, because we can't live without it and we can live better with more of it. Let's refer back to Wallace Wattles, "the fact remains that it is not possible to live a really complete or successful life unless one is rich". Amen, brother!

Please get the clear in your head that money is just a thing we use to get what we want. The emotional value we give it is totally dependent on just that, our emotions. We feel good about it when we have a lot and feel bad about it when we don't. It's all a bunch of head trash. We even give it funny names to express our feelings surrounding it and sound cool: The All-Mighty Dollar!, cash, cabbage, clams, bread, dough, bacon, cheddar, (I'm getting hungry), bankroll, stash, Benjamins, C-notes, smack, bills, wampum, moolah, treasure, pittance, and so much more.

If money is only a value stamped on old jeans, then what's all the fuss? Well, because sometimes we feel it can be hard to come by, we don't have enough, we can't get it when we need it, or the opposite, we have more than we know what to do with and need to find a way to protect it from thieves or the government. Some would say they are the same, but let's not dive into that rat's nest right now either.

For many, money is a source of frustration, aggravation, and argument, as evidenced by divorce rates in America. According to marriage.com, the top 3 reasons for divorce are infidelity, money, and lack of communication. Arguments over money in the home are a major contributing factor in the divorce rate.

"Everything from different spending habits and financial goals to one spouse making considerably more money than the other, causing a power struggle can strain a marriage to the breaking point. "Money really touches everything. It impacts people's lives," said Emmet Burns, brand marketing director for SunTrust. Clearly, money and stress do seem to go hand in hand for many couples. Financial troubles can be categorized as one of the biggest causes of divorce, following infidelity, the number one reason for divorce."

https://www.marriage.com/advice/divorce/10-most-common-reasons-for-divorce/

Since the end of World War II, the divorce rate in America had been rising, until very recently. It can be assumed that since the divorce rate was about 50% for baby boomers, born between WWII and 1964, much of the reason is that they struggled to move up from the bottom two levels of Maslow's pyramid, basic survival and safety. Millennials and Gen-Xers, born after approximately 1965, on the other hand, are securing their basic needs first, playing the field for a while, testing the waters, and making a more informed commitment when they do choose to marry. This would allow them to enter into the sacred contract of marriage with greater confidence and financial stability.

"Unlike baby boomers who married young regardless of their circumstances, millennials – and some Gen Xers – are choosing to marry once they have completed their education, have established their careers and have sound finances."

https://www.weforum.org/agenda/2018/10/divorce-united-states-dropping-because-millennials/

Now you know that money is simply a tool we use to get what we want and to argue over for divorce. What would happen if you decided to look at money differently? What would happen if you decided to 'Luvz Money'? For a moment, take a look at how you view money, where those views come from, and whether they serve you well.

I Luvz Money Exercise: What is money?

What is money to you?

What phrases about money did you grow up with?

Think hard about your parent's beliefs surrounding money.

Did you unconsciously adopt some of their beliefs?

Have these thoughts helped or hindered you?

CAN YOU REALLY LUVZ MONEY?

"If you love money, own it. The more money you have, the more you can give away. Money also buys resources, such as more time to help more people. If you've got to slave away at a minimum wage job for the rest of your life to make ends meet, how much can you really help others when you can barely help yourself?"

~ https://www.financialsamurai.com

As a child, whenever I said I love something, my father was good about correcting me with, "You can't love things. You can only love people." I think he was very right about that. So, for our purposes here, I don't actually mean that I love money, at least not in any romantic sense. Along the same token, so my religious friends don't get all up in my face, I am not implying here that we should worship money either. Money is only a thing and it certainly isn't my God. It's a tool and to say that I love money means many things on many levels. I can desire it. I can work for it. I can give it and I can receive it. I can trade it for things that I need or want. But, I can never really love it.

Can money buy happiness? No, but it can buy things that cause us to be happier and make our lives more enjoyable or fulfilling. Vacations, vehicles, homes, toys, retirement funds, experiences, ice cream, and the joy on someone's face when they receive it from you.

"I ain't rich, but I damn sure wanna be

Working like a dog all day, ain't working for me

I wish I had a rich uncle that'd kick the bucket

And that I was sitting on a pile like Warren Buffett

I know everybody says

Money can't buy happiness

But it could buy me a boat, it could buy me a truck to pull it

It could buy me a Yeti 110 iced down with some silver bullets

Yeah, and I know what they say

Money can't buy everything

Well, maybe so,

But it could buy me a boat"

~ Chris Janson "Buy me a boat"

Unfortunately, I believe that the people who say you can't buy happiness fall into one of two categories; those who don't have any and believe they never will, and those who have plenty but use it unwisely or spend more time with their money than they do with their family. Just sayin', if you have a bunch of money and you're not happy, give it to me and that will make you feel better. I promise to give it a good home.

There are those who will use the Bible to tell you that "money is the root of all evil" and the desire to become rich is against God's will.

1 Timothy 6:9-11 New Living Translation (NLT)

> 9 But people who long to be rich fall into temptation and are trapped by many foolish and harmful desires that plunge them into ruin and destruction.
>
> 10 For the love of money is the root of all kinds of evil. And some people, craving money, have wandered from the true faith and pierced themselves with many sorrows.

I will argue this point in much greater detail in a later book, but for now, let me just tell you I don't believe the apostle Paul meant in his letter to Timothy that it is godly to be poor, but that seeking money above all else, and especially loving money above God's commandments is surely not the righteous path. My contention is that God does not want you to be poor and that by being rich you are better able to fulfill his commandments. I'll leave it there for now.

Getting back to what my father taught about loving things, I believe you can love money, and God, and people, and your dog or cat, if you keep the words 'love' and 'money' in a proper perspective. Even the title of this book, 'I Luvz Money' is spelled funny to keep it playful. When you get paid for all your hard work, I want you to be able to say out loud, "I LUVZ MONEY!" in a fun and playful way. I want you to be able to shout it from the rooftops without feeling guilty. I want you to go to the store and buy something expensive and extravagant while saying to the cashier, "I LUVZ MONEY!" and make them smile. I also want you to be able to write a big fat check to your favorite charity or church and say the same thing when you hand it over. I do every time I donate to something worthwhile and I thank God for my ability to make enough money that I can give some away to help others.

Come on with me now. Say it loud and proud. "I LUVZ MONEY!"

I Luvz Money Exercise: "I LUVZ MONEY!"

Let's start a mental shift. Every time you receive money say, "I LUVZ MONEY!" out loud. That's right, loud and proud, wherever you are at the moment. Every time you spend money say, "I LUVZ MONEY!" with the same energy and enthusiasm. Do it with a playful voice and make people around you giggle a little. Give a little prayer of thanks for the ability to give and receive.

Does it sound crazy or stupid to you?

Trust me, it's not, just play along and see how you feel.

Shout out loud, "I LUVZ MONEY!"

WHY IS IT SO HARD TO TALK ABOUT MONEY?

"As a millennial, I feel as if one of the most taboo topics to discuss with one another is our finances. Sure, we may say, "Oh, I can't go out tonight. I'm broke until next paycheck," or "Let me see how much I have in my account" before committing to something, but how often do we truly discuss our finances?"

https://www.elitedaily.com/money/reasons-why-i-wont-discuss-my-finances/1832956

When I was a child, I don't remember talking about money with my parents. How much an item cost, or the utility bills, was just not something they never encouraged. All I knew about the cost of a toy or activity that I wanted was that we could or could not afford it at this time. My parents simply never talked about money in front of us children as though it was something we couldn't understand or it was an adult conversation and we weren't worthy of participating in the discussion. I never knew how much my parents made, what they had for investments, how much the electric bill was, or where they found the money to put me through college. These subjects, as we would say in German, were simply verboten.

As a matter of consequence, when I went to college and subsequently had my own apartment, I had no idea what bills to expect or how much they would cost. Auto insurance, electric bills, renters insurance, heating bills, and so much more were a total shock to me. When I tried to bring these up with my parents, the usual response was usually, "I told you these things were expensive." No, you really didn't and that's not really very helpful, thank you.

This family dynamic around money continued all the way through my mother's death at 87 and until the time I needed to take over my father's financial matters and business interests about 4 years later when he was 85. By then, he was beginning to spend down his savings and retirement investments. I discovered that he not only failed to include me in his financial matters for over 50 years, but he was also unreasonably suspicious of anyone else handling his money. He had a completely uncoordinated selection of bookkeepers and financial advisors that was designed to make sure nobody, including himself, actually knew what was going on.

When he passed at 87, I became the executor of the will and administrator of the estate. I spent the two years prior to that hiring a new bookkeeper and CPA to try to put all of his information into a unified whole where I could manage his estate in the end without total chaos. Mostly, this was accomplished and he was shocked that I could save him on taxes he was overpaying. Even still, after his passing was announced, there were small investments I had never heard of that came out of nowhere. Some of these I believe he forgot he had or didn't realize they were a death benefit, such as the Army death benefit he surely forgot about since he left the service in 1955 and another from a job he retired from in 1992.

Because my father wouldn't talk about money with his children and, it seems, was a bit paranoid about talking openly with any of the financial assistants he hired, it took me almost three years to bring it all together and close his estate properly. My younger brother will never know the hell I went through trying to settle his part of the inheritance, but that's OK. What are big brother's for anyway, right?

With our six children, we play this money game very differently. When our first three were in elementary school, we took a summer and learned some basic construction. The project was to build a treehouse. They would learn how to draw plans, do simple math, measure, use some tools, and paint. For elementary school kids, this was a really fun way to keep education alive for a summer. The treehouse stands ten feet off the ground and is 8 feet wide by 16 feet long with a front porch that wraps around a very old split-leaf oak tree. For kids that were about 7, 9, and 11, this was an ambitious project that took months to complete. The best part was when I told them they had to raise the money to buy all the lumber. WHAT!?

Yup, they needed to come up with the cash to fund this idea. We set a budget of $500 based on the price of lumber at the time and how much we thought we would need. It cost much more once we got into exterior siding and metal roofing, but they needed to cover the basic framing. At first, they totally freaked when they heard the price of wood, but then they got excited about finding ways to make money. No idea was too crazy, unless it was unsafe. They hit up the grandparents for some easy cash. They did some odd jobs in the neighborhood, like spring cleanup. Before summer was over they raised all the money, some of which came from me paying them for outdoor chores, but at least they worked for it, even if they didn't quite get the concept that I paid them so they could pay me.

We shopped for wood and other supplies together. We spent most weekends working on the monster. Before winter came that year, we had a treehouse that could sleep ten kids. Over the years it had many parties and created some great memories. It's been about twelve years now and that monster project still gets sleepovers with our younger kids as well parties on occasion with our college kids. They learned many valuable lessons building it. They understand the price of lumber, also how to work towards a goal together, and how to save for something they really want.

Now, when we go on vacation, we also talk about money with all six children and don't hold back. Everyone must get involved in some way. The usual way is each of the kids needs to save enough money to buy dinner for the family one night during the vacation. Fast food junk is not allowed as a choice of restaurants. We would eat properly in a real restaurant. The first time we did this, the idea was met with some serious whining and gnashing of teeth for months. We planned a trip to Disney World and every time we went out for dinner leading up to the trip, the kids got to look at the bill so they would understand how much dinner out costs. There were several times they wanted to cancel the vacation, but I explained the tickets were non-refundable, so get saving. Again, back to begging the grandparents and odd jobs.

As it turned out, this was a terrific experience. We took their hard-earned vacation money and purchased American Express gift cards. Whatever might be left over after buying dinner, was all theirs to use for shopping. At dinner, whoever was paying got to choose where we ate and if their budget could afford appetizers or dessert. They also got final approval if the meals we chose fit into their budget. They felt very mature and proud when the check was handed to them and they paid the server with their own credit cards. In the end, it was a fantastic lesson that we continue with today when we travel as a family. By the way, dinner for eight is not cheap.

Going through exercises like these help our children to understand the value of money and the rising expense of items. Nothing about money is off the table in our house. There are days when our kids will ask about my workday and how much I made in sales. Being self-employed, there are no guaranteed paychecks. This is not rude in our home. We celebrate each other's wins. There are days when our kids will come home and brag about their paychecks, or cry, depends. They may sell items on social media and we congratulate them on a good sale. If they earn a raise at work, we all know how much and we may go out to celebrate. There have also been times when money was in short supply, so we know how to cut back as a team in the tough times.

The point in relating these stories is to hopefully give you some ideas for ways to open up about money with your own family and to impress upon you the idea that if you keep money a secret, your children will struggle and feel awkward talking about it. If you make money part of your daily interaction, no secrets, everything on the table, then money becomes a part of life that all feel comfortable with. Think about the adult children who sheepishly need to bring up the conversation about being down on their luck and needing a 'loan' from their parents to cover the rent. How much heartache and torment goes into that awkward conversation. Since money is just another topic and tool in our home, our kids have no stress telling anyone in the family that their paycheck was smaller than expected and they need to borrow some cash, or it's a few days until payday and they need help with gas money. Anyone who is able is ready to pitch in when there is a true need. We are also quick to say no when they are looking to make a foolish purchase. For play money and play expenses, everyone knows they need to save and not ask.

If money is a taboo subject in your home, it will always be a source of stress, confusion, and conflict. If money is just another conversation about a tool you use or even a bit of friendly competition, then it becomes a game and a family event. Don't keep money a secret. Just for full disclosure, our electric bill this July 2019, is $516.26, up from $367.13 in June because everyone has the A/C plugged into their bedrooms (July has been crazy hot!), and they know it. They are not responsible for paying for it, but they understand how their usage affects the bill.

When you learn to Luvz Money, you share that love and knowledge with your family.

I Luvz Money Exercise: Talking About Money

Are there money topics you feel uncomfortable discussing with other people?

Where do those feelings come from?

What are some ways that you can begin taking about money openly and honestly with your friends or family?

If you have children, how could you help them to begin understanding money, budgets, saving, investing, and debt?

If you have a spouse, do you cooperate in planning the budget, expenditures, and setting goals for the future?

WHAT DOES IT MEAN TO BE RICH?

"I've been rich and I've been poor, and rich is better." — Mae West

Some will ask, "why did you write a book about money? Why measure riches in dollars, alone?" Some will believe, and rightly so, that there are other forms of riches more desirable than money. Yes, there are riches which cannot be measured in terms of dollars, but there are millions of people who will say, "Give me all the money I need, and I will find everything else I want." ~ NAPOLEON HILL - THINK AND GROW RICH

If you asked anyone, "Would you like to be rich?", most likely 100% would say yes. But, ask them what it means to be rich and you will get as many different answers as the number of people you ask. Every person's definition or vision of what they feel is rich is vastly different and changes with age. Ask a teen what "rich" means and they may give you a very good description of their favorite athlete or celebrity who has dozens of cars and mansions. Ask a grandmother what rich means to her, and she may tell you it's having enough money to travel and see the grandchildren whenever she wants to.

What's interesting is to ask a billionaire if they feel they are rich and see what response you get. Many of them would give you the same answers. After a certain point, money is just money with varying numbers of zeros at the end. The people remain the same with the same needs and desires. The rest is just stuff and zeros.

Side note: There are only a little over 2000 billionaires in the world as of March 2019 and the number has dropped since the previous year.
https://www.forbes.com/billionaires/#110313e4251c

According to a 2019 Modern Wealth Survey from Charles Schwab, Americans reported needing an average of $2.3 million in personal net worth to be identified as wealthy.

https://money.usnews.com/money/personal-finance/family-finance/articles/are-you-rich-how-the-wealthy-are-defined

In the United States, it takes a household net worth of $6.8 million to join the maligned and admired 1% club. It's hard to argue you're not rich once you're wealthier than 99% of your peers. On a global scale, being in the top 1% wealth becomes more attainable. All you need is an annual income of $32,000. The average laborer in Ghana would have to work 200 years to earn $32,000. This highlights the huge income (and cost of living) gap between countries.

https://www.supermoney.com/much-money-take-considered-rich-us/

So, it looks like you can celebrate because most people in the US reading this book belong to the top 1% in the world. Congratulations! Kick back and crack open a can of American champagne - that's Miller High Life, for those who didn't get it. Another of my mother's favorite sayings, "Champagne taste on a beer budget".

Now, about you...what would it take for you to consider yourself rich? How many zeros would it take? Let's not get too philosophical here. Could you actually tell me how much money it would take for you to consider yourself rich? Apparently, this a very difficult question to answer and there are many reasons why.

Recently, I asked my friends on Facebook what it would take for them to be rich and I got some very typical responses: happiness, freedom, never have to work again, do what you want when you want, having enough to give to all my family members, and more like that. Can you guess what I didn't get? Not one person could name a dollar figure that would make them feel rich. Not shocked. It's a very difficult question to put a dollar amount on. By the way, this is one of my favorites from the list, "Money only gets things not happiness granted you could buy a boat have you ever seen a sad person on a boat". Sorry, but Aaron doesn't use proper punctuation in his comments and I copied it exactly. Millennials!

This is such a tough question for so many people, mainly because they have never had the chance to experience what it means to be rich. If you have never been rich, then your best interpretation of what that could feel like may come from movies or television. We live rich lives vicariously through our celebrity idols. 'Keeping up with the Kardashians' is one of the highest-rated shows because they allow us to live their rich lives with them for an hour or so every week. Here is where I would add some very strong caution. This is meant to be entertainment. Just in case you weren't aware, reality TV isn't really real. I know! What a shock! Most of these programs are heavily scripted to ensure the correct dramatic effect. Sorry to burst your bubble, but that's the truth, folks.

In Part 3 of this book, I'll give you my explanation for what it means to be rich and we will outline a strategy together for getting you there. By the way, having or making lots of money doesn't necessarily mean you are rich. I know some very wealthy poor people. It's about scale. If your mansion and Ferrari are being repossessed, that's just a higher level of poverty.

I Luvz Money Exercise: What does it mean to be rich?

What does begin rich mean to you?

Be as specific as possible.

Write or draw a picture of what you would look like as a rich person.

How much money would you have?

What kind of material possessions would you have?

What would you do with all your riches?

How would you benefit your community?

WHY DO YOU WANT TO BE RICH?

"No one benefits from you being poor.

And no amount of depriving yourself of wealth will ever bring others to a greater level of wealth themselves. The best thing you can do for your own life and for those around you is to be abundant – in all aspects of your life."

~ Yuri Elkaim, pro soccer player

Simon Sinek in "Start with Why" makes an excellent point that to be successful, everything needs to start with your WHY. Of course, in his book, he's looking at this from the perspective of sales and introducing your business to others. It's related to the statement that 'nobody cares how much you know until they know how much you care'. Most businesses and salespeople begin with WHAT they have to sell when they should begin with WHY someone would want to do business with them. This is never more true than in the world of consultative sales. The salespeople who are best at selling high-end, very expensive equipment that require lots of consultation, patience, and many proposals, know very well that you need to begin with WHY the customer needs your product before you can explain WHAT you have and HOW it will solve their issues. It's an excellent point and I think it relates very well to our subject of money and your personal goals.

Why do you want to be rich? The answer to this question will lead to the HOW next. I think it makes sense that we don't truly know WHERE to begin or HOW to get started until we know WHY we want to be rich in the first place, but answering that question can be difficult for most people.

Can someone become rich without knowing why they want to? Yes. But accidental riches are not very common. The rich aunt who surprisingly leaves all her wealth to the one nephew who never asked her for a penny is a great story, but not many of us will experience that in our lifetime. Lottery winners or a poor hiker who stumbles onto a vein of gold make the news, but that reality doesn't happen every day. Or, maybe a mountain man from the Ozarks…

"Come and listen to my story about a man named Jed

A poor mountaineer, barely kept his family fed,

And then one day he was shootin at some food,

And up through the ground come a bubblin crude.

Oil that is, black gold, Texas tea.

Well the first thing you know ol Jed's a millionaire,

The kinfolk said "Jed move away from there"

Said "Californy is the place you ought to be"

So they loaded up the truck and they moved to Beverly

Hills, that is. Swimmin pools, movie stars."

~ The Beverly Hillbillies - source: https://www.lyricsondemand.com/tvthemes/beverlyhillbillieslyrics.html

For the real people, like you and me, we need to identify WHY we want to be rich, then create a plan for HOW it will happen and

WHAT we need to accomplish this. Sounds easy, right? It's not and that's why about 80% of people never fulfill their dream of becoming rich, but you can, if you have a strong enough why.

Let's talk about your why and develop a good reason for you to say, "I Luvz Money!".

I Luvz Money Exercise: Why?

Ask yourself why you want to be rich?

Seriously, think about it for a moment and put it into words.

What would you do with tons of money?

Would you be selfish, altruistic, philanthropic, greedy, generous, paranoid, or outrageous?

What would you look like as a person who has all the money they could ever want?

Part One Summary

YOU MUST SEE IT IN HD

"Dad. I need new glasses so I can see the TV in HD."

~ my daughter, Morgan

In order to Luvz money, you will need to see what it is and how it can be used in absolute clarity. Like my daughter says, "See it in HD".

Get certain in your mind money is not something evil. Money is simply a tool made from cotton/paper that we use to get what we want or need. Think of it as something fun to get and give. Use the phrase "I Luvz Money!" whenever you interact with it.

Talk about money with your kids. Share openly and honestly, without bragging or complaining. Take the emotion out of money talk, unless it's excitement. Don't give it some power or value other than the fact that it is something we all need to understand better.

Get crystal clear on what it would take for you to become independently wealthy and how that would affect your life.

Get serious about why you want to be rich. In order to own the "I Luvz Money!" attitude, you will need to internalize it and honestly feel you deserve it.

PART TWO
THE MONEY MINDSET

"When you begin to understand that you are a unique creature on this planet who has the ability to become anything you can envision, anything you want to be, then you must also come to the realization that this is only possible through the attainment and correct utilization of money. Money is the tool that allows you to design and live your life the way you dream it can be. I don't care what you want to be, do, or have, it is only possible to achieve that with enough money. As soon as you accept this as fact and learn to treat money as your friend, you can begin to become rich."

~ Matthew Randall

OPPORTUNITIES ARE ENDLESS, OR ARE THEY?

"Opportunity favours the bold – this is a lesson that I learned early on, and have used to guide the Virgin story. If somebody offers you an amazing opportunity but you are not sure you can do it, say yes – then learn how to do it later!"

~ *Sir Richard Branson, Virgin Group*

Why would Sir Richard say to go for it, even when you may not have the confidence, skills, or education to take on a new opportunity when it is presented? Because he understands better than most that opportunities are fleeting. Here one day and gone the next. Take them when you can. Will there be more? Yes, but not the same. Times change. You change. You get older. You move. The economy shifts. This is where I would say that opportunities are not necessarily endless, but that they are an endless changing selection of opportunities. It may be more appropriate to say that opportunities are fleeting.

I have trained in martial arts since July of 1981. I was never an athlete before I started training and would be more aptly described as a short skinny kid with glasses. Tournaments were required twice a year and I never won a single medal until I earned my black belt. Something changed after that. I began to enjoy competition and got the crazy idea that I would compete regionally and nationally. Call me a late bloomer, but I eventually qualified for the US TaeKwonDo Team at the age of 23 when most competitive athletes were being groomed and selected in their teens.

I have been very fortunate to compete for the United States in three World Championships. These were very expensive trips that involved travel to training camps, special uniforms, team warm-up suits, entry fees, hotels, meals, etc. For those who are unaware, the United States government does not financially support athletes. Many other countries will support their teams with federal funding and some (mostly the communist governments) will fully support their 'amateur athletes' to train full-time for competitions. The United States doesn't give any federal money to athletes, so all the World Championships and Olympic events you see on TV are funded by the athletes themselves and generous donations from private organizations, but mostly family and friends. The same was true in my case.

For all 3 World Championships that I competed in, I worked full-time at my martial arts academy, trained for competition in my spare time on the weekends traveling to training camps, and raised funds along the way to pay for the trips. Thankfully some of my family and friends were very generous, but we also sold program booklets, advertisements in the booklets, and put donation cans on countertops. Each member of our team needed to raise many thousands of dollars just for travel expenses. It was almost a solid year of preparation and fundraising to be able to compete, but we made it happen. All of this was after spending time and money traveling to qualifying events and competing just to be selected for the team.

This story has three points to it. First, we wanted it so badly that we were willing to do anything and make any sacrifice to make it happen. Second, we had the opportunities available to raise the funds. Third, if I didn't take the opportunity to compete when it was presented, I would have missed it entirely. And, now for the rest of the story…

1989 I was competing for the US TaeKwonDo Team at the 7th World TaeKwonDo Championships in Montreal, Canada. During a break between competitions, I had the great fortune to run into the Founder of TaeKwonDo, General Choi Hong Hi, in the lobby of our hotel. He was gracious enough to sit with me and a few teammates in the lobby for some conversation. This is a rare event as I was low ranking on the list of black belts and he was a busy and important man always in demand. I will be forever grateful that he spent this time with me as I learned a very valuable lesson that took me about ten more years to fully understand. The teacher was ready, the student was not.

At one point in our conversation, General Choi invited me to compete for the United States TaeKwonDo team again in the First Soviet World Championships. At first, of course, I was extremely flattered and stunned that he would extend this invitation to me personally. When I asked about the details, he said it would be held in less than twelve months, in Uzbekistan! My brain went into overload thinking about the timeframe, the expenses, the fact that we just spent the past year fundraising, would need to do it all over again, would need to beg family and friends for more money, would need to sacrifice more family time training…so, naturally, I blurted out without thinking, "Sir, I'm not sure I could afford to make that commitment". He laughed, immediately, and responded with, "You are American! What do you worry about money?" "Yes, Sir. I will do my best" was all I could manage at that time to get myself out of a very embarrassing hole and that was the end of our conversation.

I was furious and confused all at once. Does he think all Americans just have money lying around? After Montreal, it was back to the camps and begging for more money. This time, my business was growing and I was able to support myself better, but still, there was more needed and Uzbekistan was much farther away than Canada, so the expenses were about double. There was also the thought that in just two more years, 1992 would be the 8th World Championships in Korea, and that was the big prize. To compete for gold in the birthplace of TaeKwonDo would be amazing. The fundraising machine would never stop.

Now, we can cut to the chase...the fundraising and training continued. I raised all the necessary funds. In 1990, I competed in the First Soviet World Championships winning a bronze medal. In 1992, I competed in Korea, winning the Gold. It was such an incredible journey that I will never forget and might tell you about in a future book. What does this have to do with money and opportunity?

General Choi was very wise and very correct. I am an American and money is all around me. It may not be in my pocket at this time, but opportunities are abundant. Not every country, or even every area of ours, has the same opportunities available, however. I know, and have traveled to, many countries where there is such extreme poverty that there are no opportunities, no money, no support, no freedoms, and the people are where they are and will stay there without any hope of ever improving their lives. They live day-to-day just trying to survive and don't even know why. There are places in the world where there simply is no opportunity to earn money and improve one's financial situation beyond basic living necessities.

I have also traveled to places, such as Uzbekistan during the Soviet regime, where there is education, food, and employment (because it's required for everyone to have a job), but there is no hope of leaving or improving your life because the government will not allow it. We stopped in Moscow first before flying south and I asked our translator about the people who travel outside the country for work. How do they feel when they return? (they have to return or be hunted down by the government) The answer was very short and with true sadness, "All they do is drink".

My point in this lengthy story is that here in the United States, we are surrounded by endless opportunity and abundance. I was able to raise funds for very expensive training and trips to three World Championships because I had the desire to do so and the will to take action. At the time, I was so wrapped up in training and fundraising that I didn't stop to recognize just how lucky I was to be born in a place of abundant opportunity. Later in life, I would meet people who came to this country as immigrants looking for a better life than what they could find in their home country. They worked hard and some made plenty of money. These opportunities were simply not available in their birthplaces. It took me at least ten years after the conversation with General Choi to look back and realize just how fortunate I am to be surrounded by money and the ability to make as much as I want, as long as I'm willing to put in the effort. He was right, I'm American. Why should I worry about money? On the other hand, for some kid living in the dumps of some backwater swamp or the barrios of a big city, it's very hard to look past the immediate needs for food, clothing, and shelter, and see all the opportunities that lie like diamonds at their feet.

"But everywhere we see rich and poor living side by side, in the same environment, and often engaged in the same vocations. When two people are in the same locality and in the same business, and one gets rich while the other remains poor, it shows that getting rich is not primarily a matter of environment. Some environments may be more favorable than others, but when two people in the same

business are in the same neighborhood and one gets rich while the other fails, it indicates that getting rich is the result of doing things in a certain way.

And further, the ability to do things in this certain way is not due solely to the possession of talent, for many people who have great talent remain poor, while others who have very little talent get rich.

Studying the people who have gotten rich, we find that they are an average lot in all respects, having no greater talents and abilities than other people have. It is evident that they do not get rich because they possess talents and abilities that others do not have, but because they happen to do things in a certain way."

~ Wallace D. Wattles, 'The Science of Getting Rich'

How is it that one person, raised in a solid middle-class home can learn to play the guitar in a way that speaks to your soul and would bring tears to your eyes, yet makes a meager living as a music teacher, while another who grew up on the streets of Harlem and can play adequately, but not great, ends up on a record label making millions of dollars?

Can I be perfectly honest with you? Thanks. When I was selected for the US TaeKwonDo Team, there were other athletes around the country who were younger and better than me. Yes, it's true. Taller and better looking also, but, hey, whatever. The difference is that I saw the opportunities and took them when they did not. Yes, I still needed to qualify, and I worked very hard, but others who also qualified refused the opportunities saying they couldn't raise the funds or take the time. They lacked the desire and vision. I simply wanted it more than they did.

If you haven't seen the movie "Yes, Man" yet, I would encourage you to do that. Jim Carrey's character, Carl, is a man who doesn't want to take opportunities. He lives a dull and depressing life where he actively avoids doing anything interesting, hates his job, turns down invitations to go out with friends, and lives a totally unremarkable life by choice. Until...one day he happens upon a motivational seminar where the speaker pressures him into a challenge that he has to say "YES!" to every opportunity presented, no matter how crazy. I won't spoil it any further in case you haven't seen it, but let's just say that it's a life-changing event for him, in a good way. I would wish that upon you, that you take advantage of opportunities and make changes in your life that will rock you to the very core.

How about you? Are you ready to take on new opportunities? Do you have enough desire and vision to become rich? Do you want it bad enough? I will say this often, and it's true, if I can do it, you can, too. I'm not remarkable and you don't need to be either to become rich. You just need to want it bad enough to take chances, get messy, and fail a few times.

I Luvz Money Exercise: Opportunities

What opportunities have you had?

What opportunities did you pass on?

What opportunities did you try and how did they turn out?

What did you learn from all of these experiences?

Is there an opportunity that has been presented to you at this time?

If so, what would happen if you take advantage of it?

IT'S ALL IN YOUR HEAD

"Every thought of yours is a real thing - a force"

~ Prentice Mulford (1834-1891)

"It's all in your head" is another of my mother's favorite sayings. For a woman who's education was interrupted in the sixth grade by a little thing called World War II, and was never able to return to formal schooling, and learned English as a second language on her own, she was amazingly perceptive and didn't even know it. I was well into my twenties before I realized she was right, it is all in my head.

What mom meant by "It's all in your head" was everything is based on perception. Actually, I'm giving her a little too much credit here. She really meant, "You're crazy", but my therapist says I need to move on, so let's go forward. Whenever I was sad, depressed, angry, or thinking I couldn't do something, she would say "It's all in your head". That just made me feel worse most of the time, but I think she knew me well enough that it would also make me more determined. My normal response would be "No, it's not!" and I would get to work proving her wrong. Looking back, I have so many successes to thank my mother for, because she told me I couldn't do it, or I was crazy, or it was impossible, or it was "all in your head" that I accepted these are challenges just to prove her wrong.

Case in point, when my mother and her family were being chased out of Prussia by the Russian army, that left a lasting impression. When I told my mom that I was selected to compete in the First Soviet World Championships and would travel to Moscow, she was terrified. She tried to talk me out of it because she actually believed that they would keep me and never let me leave. Since the Russians imprisoned her mother for two years, why wouldn't she think it could happen to me, except that 50 years had passed and much changed over that time. I committed to the trip, raised the funds, and took home a bronze medal mostly to prove that mom and many others were totally wrong about me. Looking back, it was a silly reason, but the experience was amazing.

"The beliefs you truly hold, the ones you've decided to believe, your faith, will cause you to create or attract the experiences which will verify them. When you change your beliefs, your experiences will change."

~ Harry Palmer, founder of Avatar EPC

In order to become rich, you must first make a shift in mindset (clever, don't you think, how I avoided saying 'change') around your thoughts on money. I'm talking about at the core level. To do that, you must examine your true and honest-to-God beliefs about money. Let's dig deeper into the head trash to see what is useful, what can be recycled, and what needs to go to the curb.

Harry Palmer, in the Avatar EPC book series, makes a good point that we are all products of our experiences, but we will often interpret these experiences based on ideas that have been forced upon us by others. These are not necessarily original thoughts that we created and accepted on our own, but rather core beliefs that have been given to us by parents, mentors, political parties, friends, teachers, religious leaders, and others during particularly impressionable times in our lives. Anthony Robbins may also add that NLP, NeuroLinguistic Programming, can play a part in developing our belief system. Still others in psychology will assert that the environment has a large effect on our belief system.

The point is that we hold on to many core beliefs that may or may not serve us well. Many of these beliefs are so deep that we don't even remember where they came from. Even worse, we never take the time to examine if they were created by us or given to us. We simply take it for granted that they are part of our world. I find it to be very valuable when I have a strong feeling about something, like money, to take a moment and ask if this is my feeling, did I create it, and does it make my life better? If not, then it's head trash and goes to the curb. I then get to go shopping for a new thought about the situation that will serve me better.

How does this relate to money? The next time you have a major purchase to make, maybe a television, a car, a vacation, moving to a new home or apartment, etc., take a moment to assess your feelings surrounding that purchase. Does it give you excitement or anxiety? Keep in mind that the product and the money associated with it don't have any feelings or stake in the game. Any feelings you have in making this purchase come from within, but are they your feelings and do they serve you well? Do you hear your mother's or father's word coming out of your mouth? Are you reacting out of habit or by design? Any way you look at it, "It's all in your head". The question is, do these thoughts and feelings help you or hinder you?

As an example, when we first had children, I remember saying things to our son from instinct that my parents said to me. The words just came out of my mouth and sometimes I regretted them. On occasion, my wife would say that I sound like my father. Sometimes, I would hear my mother's voice in my head. An internal audit was necessary to determine if these thoughts and words were my own or something I learn from my parents, were they still relevant, and did I want to continue to think and speak that way? This is the same process we also need to go through when we approach the subject of money.

What experiences do you or your family have around money? What words do you use when you talk about money? I'm referring to the everyday stuff of life, not the sit-down with a financial advisor kind, but simple and common conversations such as, "Can we go out for dinner and a movie?" How do these conversations make you feel? Are the thoughts and words coming from your own creation and experience or do they come from programming deep in your past? Do they still serve you well or are they holding you back?

Be honest with yourself as you think of these questions and situations. Every time you find you are making an excuse for why you think a certain way, stop and ask again if these thoughts and feelings are really your own. There are no excuses allowed in this exercise, only honest truths. It's happening inside your head, so who cares and stopping judging yourself. Just ask honestly. Anytime you want or need some good honesty, ask your spouse or best friend what phrases you use consistently when you talk about money and who they think you sound like. You may get some brutal answers. And, if you are really into punishment, ask a kid.

Before we discuss in the next chapter how 'lack' and 'abundance' thinking affect your world, take a moment to write down how you feel, what you say, and what you do in a situation where you truly do not have enough cash on hand to buy or do what you want?

I Luvz Money Exercise: It's all in your head

What kind of head trash are you carrying around?

How is it serving you, good or bad?

If you were to let go of some of the head trash, what would you throw away?

What would change in your life if you did throw it away?

ABUNDANCE VS LACK

"If you do not have enough, it is because you are stopping the flow of money coming to you, and you are doing that with your thoughts. You must tip the balance of your thoughts from lack-of-money to more-than-enough-money. Think more thoughts of abundance than of lack, and you have tipped the balance."

~ Rhonda Byrne, 'The Secret'

What is abundance and what is lack? Very simply put, abundance thinking is looking at the world as full of opportunity and lack thinking is the opposite, seeing the world for what it is missing, lacking, where it falls short, etc. These are the Yin and Yang of life. Life truly does have both abundance and lack. We have floods and droughts, desserts and oceans, grasslands and rainforests, but as you are a person living with an amazing and powerful mind, we have the ability to choose to see the world in the way that we desire. The secret to becoming rich is to choose abundance over lack as often as possible.

The secret to abundance thinking is truly all in your head, just as the secret to lack thinking is. Let's start with a hard look at the words we use surrounding money, not the phrases we learned as a child, but the words we use daily that form our opinions about money. The language we choose has true power. Our thoughts form words and those words once uttered create a certain energy that surrounds us, our actions, and what we attract. In a very real sense, the words we let fall from our mouths can attract money or repel it.

"Can we go out for dinner and a movie tonight?" Assume, for the moment that your significant other asks this question and you actually have only $11.38 in your wallet. The other person has $5.79. Between the two of you, there is $17.17. Probably not enough for dinner and a movie. That is a hard reality for this moment in time. I've been there and completely understand the feeling. In the past, my first reaction would be a very common one, "We don't have enough." A fair, accurate, and very honest statement.

"We don't have enough." What happens when you put that energy out to the universe? Simply put, the universe will confirm this as your reality and work to ensure it stays that way because that is how you think, how you picture yourself, how you believe reality is, and the universe wants you to achieve all your dreams. Every time you think or say, "I don't have enough", the universe will act accordingly to bring that into your reality because that is what you are attracting.

All day long, every thought and word we have is attracting that exact thing into our lives. If you believe that money is the route of all evil, you will see evidence of that in every news broadcast you watch. If you say that money can't buy happiness, then you will find evidence of that by reading or watching stories of rich people who are miserable. If you think that you don't have enough, then you will take action, or not, every day to ensure that you never have enough. The universe just wants you to be happy and if not having enough is what you believe, it will make sure you get exactly that.

But, but, but...the reality is that we only have $17.17 and can't afford dinner and a movie!

Let's pause there for a moment and remember some occasions in your past, or maybe present, where this type of reality happened.

How did you react? What thoughts came into your head? What words came out of your mouth? Using the example of going out for dinner and a movie, this is where a shift from lack to abundance will make a world of difference. No matter how hard you try, that $17.17 isn't instantly going to change into $50 or $100, but we can instantly change our mindset and energy surrounding it. Let's change, "We don't have enough…" (negative, lack) to "Maybe tonight it would be better to eat in and watch TV? Let's save up for dinner and a movie next week." (action, positive, abundance). Using this thought process we are creating a mindset of understanding current budgetary restrictions, which are a fact of life at this point in time, and generating positive energy with a plan for the future, which is open to all possibilities and opportunities. Take that to the next level and create a plan for ensuring there is enough for dinner and movie out every week for date night. Now, we are getting closer to a true abundance mindset and the road to riches. Maybe in a future book we will discuss buying your own restaurant and movie theatre, but let's start simple.

In another example, my teenage son just the other day asked if I would buy him another year of gaming for his Xbox. Apparently, there is only so much you can do or access for free (smart business model for Microsoft) and he needs an annual subscription to be able to play online with his friends. Now, all summer long he had opportunities to work for neighbors and friends doing lawn maintenance. He did take a few jobs and could easily have done more to earn enough to pay for his gaming membership, but he chose sleepovers and other activities instead of earning money. He chose to work only for as much as he needed at the moment and didn't plan for the future.

My response could come in multiple fashions, and each would have its own energy attached to it as well as results and consequences.

1. Sure. I'll give you $60.

2. No. I don't have $60 to give you.

3. Sorry. You had an opportunity to earn that money and didn't.

4. OK, but I'll give you home chores to pay me back.

and, I'm sure those of you who have children, or remember the days, can find a few more.

Let's look at the energy and consequences that each of these provides.

1. Positive energy, feeling of abundance for me, but teaches nothing to him and will ensure that he returns with his hand out when he needs more.

2. Negative energy, feeling of lack, teaches him that money is in scarce supply.

3. Negative energy, feeling of lack again, and punitive damage with guilt.

4. Positive energy, creating some abundance and responsibility, but it still means that the money will come out of my pocket and the sweat equity from him. At least he will earn his game time.

I chose another route in this conversation. My response was, "I will get you the membership in advance when you show me that you have enough lawn mowing jobs booked to pay me back." He immediately got on Facebook, put the word out, and got the jobs booked. He also contacted previous customers and got back on their schedules. Since he was very motivated, he earned more than the price of his membership and was very proud of his efforts. Yes, he is still 14 and complained along the way, but he was actually proud.

My son's first thought around this sudden need for money was simple and direct, go the Bank of Dad and ask for charity, not a loan, but a handout. This head trash comes from a sense of lack, not abundance. He was surrounded by opportunities that he didn't take advantage of and therefore was not prepared when the need arose. If I had just given him the money, he would have learned that money isn't something he needs to earn. Would that be different for a 6-year-old? Definitely, as he wouldn't have the same opportunities. For a 14-year-old, he can learn to earn and be proud of his efforts instead of being a beggar and feel shame for his lack. His urgency was all in his head and that prevented him from looking for the abundance of opportunities lying at his feet. If I was a better banker and negotiator, I would have charged him interest, but, hey, it got the job done and a good lesson learned.

Unfortunately, the lack mentality is so easily taught in most homes and that is why the majority of people are not as rich as they claim they would like to be. Every time we heard phrases as a child such as, "It's too expensive", "We can't afford that", or "Money doesn't grow on trees", that teaches children that there are no options, no opportunities, no resources, to make the situation better. This level of hopelessness causes people to believe that they can't improve or that if they just get by, they are doing better than their parents could. "Oh, happy day! I must be rich because I don't need to worry about paying the heating bill this month like my parents always did." Abundance mindset is so much more than basic survival.

"It (self-actualization) refers to the person's desire for self-fulfillment, namely, to the tendency for him to become actualized in what he is potentially. The specific form that these needs will take will of course vary greatly from person to person. In one individual it may take the form of the desire to be an ideal mother, in another it may be expressed athletically, and in still another it may be expressed in painting pictures or in inventions." (Maslow, 1943, p. 382–383).

As long as a person is focused simply on survival, paying the bills, living paycheck-to-paycheck, they are existing at the bottom of Maslow's Hierarchy of Needs. Abundance mindset is the ability to reach higher to the top of this scale, but one cannot do that while always struggling to satisfy the physiological and safety needs of the body. I would argue that one cannot truly love and feel a sense of belonging to their community until they can easily and without stress satisfy all their basic needs.

But does this mean that a person who is actually struggling, financially, physically, with health, with mental illness, chemical dependency, abuse, with relationships, or in other ways, cannot begin to adopt an abundance mindset? It seems that the answer is a bit of a 'chicken or egg' question. Did the lack mindset cause the current predicament, or does the current predicament prevent a person from thinking in a positive direction? I tend to believe the former, not the latter, is more often the culprit.

It was the mid-1990's and I had the brilliant idea that since one business was doing well, and I had some time on my hands, I should start another business. So that I don't bore you with details, it didn't go well. In fact, it was a disaster. Spiraling construction costs and incompetent city code enforcers caused the budget to be completely out of control and before it even really began, it failed. We lost a bundle of money which eventually would cause us to lose a home in addition. These were tough times. Lack mindset was abundant (how's that for a word twist?) in our home for a few years. No matter what we did, it seemed like we would never crawl out of the hole.

During this time, I launched myself heavily into self-help books for survival and discovered that almost all referred to abundance mindset as the secret to just about everything in life. It was then that I began to practice the principles learned in The Power of Positive Thinking, Think And Grow Rich, The Secret, As A Man Thinketh, The Science of Getting Rich, and many more. Each and every book credits an abundance mindset with success, financially and otherwise.

To finish the story, we did crawl out of that hole, learned some wonderful lessons about city politics, grew our business and got back on track financially. Abundance mindset was something I thought I understood and gave it credit for helping us get back to normal, but we still weren't rich. That was because we were only focused on 'getting back to normal', and normal is not rich. Abundance thinking is only as powerful as your imagination, and ours was very limited apparently. I was firmly back to a place where good enough was good enough, and that felt comfortable. To get rich, however, would take another giant leap in mindset.

I Luvz Money Exercise: Abundance

If there is one attitude towards money that you could change right now, what would it be?

How would your life be different if you simply stopped worrying about money and started focusing on abundance?

How have feelings and thoughts of lack hindered you in the past?

GOOD LUCK AND BAD LUCK

"Good luck is when opportunity meets preparation, while bad luck is when lack of preparation meets reality."

~ Eliyahu Goldratt, Israeli Business Management Guru

Truth! Oh, how many times I blamed my lack of success on bad luck. In reality, it was my lack of preparation, lack of faith, lack of initiative, and lack of work ethic that held me back. It was never a lack of education or opportunity. I had plenty of that. It was always me blaming the economy, the community, the city, the weather, the traffic, the timing, my mentors, my employees, my family, and just sheer dumb bad luck. Hogwash! There were times when I felt like Pooh Bear seeing heffalumps and woozles everywhere stopping me from reaching my goals. Oh, bother! That's just more head trash.

"You Make Your Own Luck"

~ Ernest Hemingway

When you realize that there is no such thing as luck, and that life is simply full of opportunities that we are ready to accept or not, then it is far easier to take control of your own life. To believe in luck is to hand over full control of your life to the wind and hope for the best. I think this is where 80% of the population exists, waiting for luck to show up and announce itself as the gift you have been praying for. "I'm here! Take me now!"

Stop waiting for 'lady luck' to drop by. Stop blaming everything that doesn't go your way on 'bad luck'. Stop giving away all your personal power. Take back your life by accepting that you are in control. Yes, God has a plan and all that, but mostly you are in charge of making the smaller decisions about your life. Will things go wrong sometimes? Certainly. Will things happen that couldn't be expected? Of course. Will you have days when it seems that absolutely nothing goes your way? Guaranteed. But, if you believe that it's all due to bad luck, then you are making yourself powerless to change the situation. It simply is what it is. Move on.

Create your own 'good luck'. Start by acknowledging that you have more power over your life than you previously believed. Get the notion of luck out of your head, make plans, do the research, do your due diligence, have a positive attitude, think in terms of possibilities. When things go awry, then that's just how it is at this moment. Minor inconveniences. Think of it as a life lesson or a closing door that opens a window. To think any differently from this is to contradict every successful author who's ever written a motivational book since, and including, Jesus. I will save this for another book, but Jesus was a motivational speaker and preached positive thinking along with prayer.

"Ask and it will be given to you; seek and you will find; knock and the door will be opened to you." - Matthew 7:7

When you stay positive, when you search for opportunities, when you keep your heart and mind open to the vast power of the universe, when you stay focused on your goals, then…you create your own luck.

"Fortune favors the prepared mind."

~ Louis Pasteur

I Luvz Money Exercise: Luck

Knowing what you know now about luck, what habits of thought and behavior might you want to adjust to attract more good fortune into your life?

THINK BIG. NO, BIGGER!

"Go after your goal obsessively, persistently, and as though your life depends on it — because it does!"

~ Grant Cardone, 'The 10X Rule'

In 'The 10X Rule' by Grant Cardone, he makes one very big point that most people are not as successful as they want to be because their goals are not big enough and their corresponding actions are not enough. While I would agree with him to a point, I'm not a huge fan of driving myself to the brink of insanity trying to take all my actions to the 10th degree. I do believe he is correct that most of us simply do not do enough, but I'm not willing to kill myself and destroy my family to get it all done and achieve some level of success. There must be some balance.

What Cardone is correct about, is that most of us have goals that are way too small and we need to think bigger, much bigger. Shoot for the stars and you may land on the moon. In this chapter, I want you to consider creating a financial goal that is much greater than you have ever contemplated. Think of something huge. Go a little crazy and dream big. Now, double that. You heard me correctly. Take that dream and double it. 10X it, if you want, but at least double it. How does that feel?

Let's assume for a moment that your big dream was a vacation home on a lake. Why not have one in the mountains also? Maybe it was a new car. Why not have a convertible sports car for the good weather and a luxury car for the rainy days. Why not make your dream bigger than you have ever dreamed of before?

Let's revisit Matthew for a moment: *"Ask and it will be given to you; seek and you will find; knock and the door will be opened to you."* - Matthew 7:7

If your ASK is small and easy to accomplish, then setting the bar low may be good for your ego, but it isn't for your bank account. Raise the bar and accept the challenge to grow beyond your current preconceived limitations. Yes, I'm going back to the notion that 'It's all in your head', and it is.

"What we refer to as our comfort zone becomes at times not quite so comfortable, as it is familiar. Old habits and behaviors that we struggle to transcend become impeded by the barriers of this comfort zone; which I now more aptly refer to as the familiar zone."

~ Mel Schwartz, https://melschwartz.com/the-familiar-zone/

We often fail to ask for something bigger out of the fear of the unknown or fear of failure. This causes us to remain in our 'comfort zone', which is more appropriately called our 'familiar zone'. It's not really that comfortable, but we stay there because it is familiar. The thing the rich do that the rest don't, is they ask for more, they want more, they do more, and they think BIGGER. That's what I'm asking you to do here.

Expand beyond what is familiar and step into what is uncomfortable. Break free from doing what you have always done and explore new worlds. Only in the space where you are uncomfortable can there be growth.

I Luvz Money Exercise: Thinking Bigger

What is a goal that you have always dreamed about, but were afraid it was too big?

What would it take for you to get there?

What's really holding you back?

If you answered money to these questions, then what would you need to change to make enough for this dream?

YOUR WHY MUST BE BIGGER THAN YOUR BUT

"Your complaints, your drama, your victim mentality, your whining, your blaming, and all of your excuses have NEVER gotten you even a single step closer to your goals or dreams. Let go of your nonsense. Let go of the delusion that you DESERVE better and go EARN it! Today is a new day!"

— *Steve Maraboli, Unapologetically You: Reflections on Life and the Human Experience*

I call it the 'Backpack Full of Excuses'. I once saw someone walking around with a backpack that had the words "I CAN DO THIS!" embroidered on it in big letters. At first, I thought that this was pretty cool, then I thought of how many of us walk around wearing this saying on our backpacks, t-shirts, hats, or whatever, and on the inside we have a long list of excuses for why we haven't done 'THIS' yet? To me, that backpack now represents an image of what I find humorous and sad at the same time.

Picture someone wearing a backpack that says "I CAN DO THIS!" and this is their declared mantra for all the world to see. When you ask them how they are going to do it or if they are getting closer to that goal, they carefully take off the backpack, set it down on the ground, unzip the larger compartment, and proceed to pull out a heavy stack of well-used laminated signs that begin with...

"Well, I just..."

"I'm not there yet, but..."

"Someday I'm gonna..."

"I almost did, but…"

"Tomorrow I'm gonna…"

"I wanted to, but…"

"I'm still hoping…"

"When _____ happens, I'm gonna…"

"The time isn't right at the moment because…"

"If only…"

"I would be there, but it's _____ fault that…"

"The economy is holding me back because…"

"I was doing great until…"

"As soon as…"

"I had a setback because…"

"I'm waiting for…"

…do you get the picture? Have you ever used the same excuses? I know I have and they held me back for years.

As long as your list of BUT's is bigger than your list of WHY's, your backpack will simply continue to grow and be a weight that keeps you from becoming the person you deserve to be.

It's time to turn over the backpack, dump it all out, recycle the paper and begin to fill it with a list of successes. When your backpack becomes so full of cards that list all of your achievements, not your excuses, then you can get a new pack that reads "I DID IT!" and wear it proudly. So, how does one make this happen?

Right now, every time you catch yourself using an excuse, turn it around and say "Day One!".

Too many people use the phrase "One day I'm gonna…". I want you to start thinking in terms of "This is Day One of me taking a small step towards that goal." Then do something immediately that you can feel good about. Make one phone call. Make a list of action steps. Make an appointment. Write one page of your new book. Drop and do 10 push-ups. Throw away that half-eaten candy bar in your hand. Make something happen, no matter how small, that will lead you one step closer to your goal, dream, desire, or picture of who you want to become.

To make this "Day One!" for any goal, you will need a good list of WHY's. Your WHY list will need to be big, strong, powerful, convincing, and unstoppable. If you want to be rich, your WHY must be so important is shakes you to the core and forces you to take action. Please review the chapter, 'Why do you want to be rich?' from Part One.

I have a friend who started in a network marketing business because he lost his business, his home, and he was living in his car. His WHY was so big that there were no BUT's left. He needed a home for his family. Because his WHY was so clear and his need was so great, he took that business and turned it into over a million dollars a year. He is now retired, in his 40's, and travels the world with his family.

For many of us, like me, suffering from Middle-Class Curse, we don't make a WHY big enough because the consequences of using

BUT's all day aren't big enough. Yes, when you are comfortable, it's easy to use BUT because nothing terrible will happen, unless you consider living life that is unfulfilled terrible. When your belly is full, your life doesn't need to be as much, so our WHY gets shoved in a closet until tragedy strikes.

Start feeling uncomfortable with your life. Start feeling unhappy with sliding along day after day. Start feeling unsatisfied with not achieving your dreams. Take your WHY's out of the closet, dust them off, set them on a shelf where you will see them every day. Start living for your WHY and never use the word BUT again.

I had a manager once tell me to put a picture of my family on my desk, in my cubicle, right next to the computer. I asked him why. He said, "so you will remember why you're hunting for sales so hard." It wasn't long after that my WHY was to leave that job because my WHY wasn't to find sales for that company, but to make a better life for my family, and it wasn't going to happen by working for them. Nice people and a great place to work, but my goals are so much bigger than making another sale for someone else.

It's time to make your list of WHY's bigger than ever before.

I Luvz Money Exercise: Making your WHY bigger

What is something to which you have said, "If only I could, but..."?

Go back and think of all the reasons why you want it, why you should have it or do it, why you need it, why you deserve it.

Make the list so long that there aren't enough BUT's to keep your WHY's from making it happen.

WHY POSITIVE AFFIRMATIONS DON'T WORK

"I am so happy and grateful now that money is coming to me in increasing amounts, through multiple sources, on a continuous basis."

~ Bob Proctor, www.ProctorGallagherInstitute.com

This positive affirmation from Bob Proctor I kept hanging in my office for many years and considered it a source of inspiration. I suppose that, if I had taken it seriously, I may have taken action towards achieving that goal much earlier in my life. It is true today, and maybe this quote had something to do with my success today, but mostly it was just a quaint thought hanging in my office that I had no idea how to accomplish.

In 'The Secret Code of Success', Noah St. John makes the point that positive affirmations don't work and I believe he is right, to a point. There are an endless number of self-help books that will teach various types of mantras or affirmations such as "I am a millionaire", "I am living in a mansion with money that just flows into my accounts daily", "I drive a brand-new Tesla and have all the money I could ever desire", etc. The problem with positive affirmations such as these is two-fold: first, they are a lie and we know it, second, we aren't taking the necessary action steps to realize these fantasies and, third, we probably don't even know how to get there.

My point is that I believe we can't lie to ourselves on the road to riches. We can, however, create more valid affirmations that will lead us to our goals. Emile Coue may have had it right in the early 1900s when he used a form of psychotherapy based on auto-suggestion. Repeatedly using phrases such as "Every day, in every way, I'm getting better and better" may prompt a person to take small steps daily towards achieving that as a reality. In fact, many of the classic American writers and motivational speakers used the 'Coue Method' as a basis for their success; Napoleon Hill, Norman Vincent Peale, Robert H. Schuller, and others.

It is my contention that positive affirmations will not work unless one understands the method by which these dreams will become reality and there is a plan in place to take daily action. Vision boards can also offer great reminders of one's desires, but unless you truly believe in your heart and soul that every day, in every way, you are making progress towards that vision, it eventually becomes a source of stress, disappointment, and a sign of personal failure.

So, now that I have beaten your dreams into an early grave, what can you do? Change your mantras, affirmations, and vision boards to reflect the actions you are willing to take towards success and the riches you desire. Change "I am a millionaire" to "What is one small thing I will do today that will help make me a millionaire in 5 years?" Now, we are thinking in terms of action and progress, not lying to ourselves. Perhaps next to your 'pie in the sky' vision board, you can create a series of boards that reflect the steps necessary to achieve that long-term vision?

If it's a Ferrari you desire, or a huge donation to some important charity, then what needs to happen by the end of this year to make some steady progress towards that goal? Take that huge goal, break it down into annual, monthly, and weekly goals until you have a manageable chunk that can be reduced to one simple daily action step. Create an action mantra (not affirmation) you can refer to all day long that includes your daily action and your long-term vision. Like the 'millionaire' example in the previous paragraph, it should be phrased as "Today I will do X to lead me one step closer to my big goal of Y in Z time." We will discuss this more in the chapter on 'Consistency' in Part Four.

Let's take those old affirmations and turn them into action plans. I know the idea of action plans makes some people cringe. Nothing happens without action. You can sit in your easy chair all day reciting affirmations, but unless you get your butt (and your but's) out the chair, it ain't gonna happen.

I Luvz Money Exercise: Turning Affirmations into Action

Write an affirmation in terms of action that you will take.

Don't waste time lying to yourself, just jot down a simple phrase that's easy to remember and includes a step you will take daily to help reach some goal.

Example: Today, I will introduce my business/product/service to one more person before the day is over.

DON'T KEEP UP WITH THE JONES', CONGRATULATE THEM

"The more you can celebrate and bless the success of those around you, the more you open yourself to receive blessings in your life." ~ Kute Blackson, https://kuteblackson.com

Congratulating others on their success is a part of your path to success. Sounds crazy, doesn't it? Everyone thinks it's all about competition. Competition mindset comes from lack. When your neighbor gets a raise at work and decides to buy a new car, congratulate them, honestly and from the heart. Give them positive energy. This comes from an abundance mindset. On the flip side, if you scorn them, are jealous of their success, and criticize them for spending money wastefully, you only damage your relationship. I think it's even worse if you congratulate them falsely and internally hope they hit that pothole of the end of the street and break a tie rod or dent a rim. This is a serious lack mindset and that energy will be reflected back to you.

When you hear people talking about the rich and famous in negative terms, tearing them down, criticizing their success, wishing they would fall off their pedestals, this only cheapens themselves personally and does nothing to harm those they ridicule. And, the higher one rises, they more people will gather to drag them down. Case in point, nobody is more vilified than the President. It doesn't matter which party they belong to, they will be torn to shreds every day in the media, by special interest groups, by the opposing party and, during election season, by their own party running to take their place. It's no wonder that they age 20 years in 8 years of office.

President Andrew Shepherd: "Sydney, seldom does a day go by where I am not burned in effigy."

~ The American President movie, 1995

It took me quite a while to begin thinking this way and celebrating the success of people more successful than I. Being naturally competitive, it was honestly difficult. I attended personal development weekend retreats where I was told that I couldn't make the progress I was looking for until I worked on being less competitive and more cooperative. "But, I'm a World Champion competitor with gold medals from foreign countries! How dare you tell me I'm too competitive. I built my business on being competitive." It took many many years to understand that this was exactly the attitude that made me a champion but was also holding me back from becoming rich.

To be competitive on the competition floor is where it belongs. To believe in life, business, and the community that 'to the victor belongs the spoils' (Sen. Wm Marcy-1832) is not going to 'win friends and influence people', as Dale Carnegie would say. To be competitive inside the ring is required to win, but outside the ring is a lack mindset. In sports, there can only be one winner, but in life, anyone and everyone willing to work hard and learn can be a winner and there are plenty of winnings to go around.

An abundance mindset allows you to congratulate and thank those who surpass you. Celebrate the success of those who rise above. An abundance mindset also encourages you to reach from on high and lend a hand to those who need it. Give back to help others rise up and possibly pass you along the way. When you stop competing and realize that there is plenty for everyone, abundance will become clear and opportunity will present itself to you everywhere you look.

How is this abundance mindset applied in real life? When you see a headline that some person or company is purchasing another company, what is your initial reaction?

"That's just not right. They'll be too big and have a monopoly."

"Another rich person getting even richer. That's so unfair."

"I wonder how many people will lose their jobs in the merger."

"I bet prices will be going up again"

"I wish I had stock in that company."

These are all lack mindset and will hold you back by surrounding yourself with negative energy and emotions. This, by the way, is not a wholly fictitious example. Just this morning I was in a business networking meeting with a friend who said his company was bought out by another making them the largest publishing company in the United States.

https://www.seacoastonline.com/zz/news/20190805/gatehouse-media-enters-into-agreement-to-acquire-gannett-forming-largest-us-publishing-company

Unfortunately, he was downsized in the process along with approximately 300 fellow employees. He remains positive and optimistic about finding future employment.

What is the lesson in this? My friend remains positive and is taking action to seek employment. He wishes the company well, understands that it's a business decision, nothing personal, and is approaching this change with an abundance mindset. As a result, he received some recommendations and referrals from those at the meeting that may help him find opportunities quickly. Others who were affected by the downsizing will approach this with a lack mindset. They will criticize the merger, complain about their bad luck, quickly run to the unemployment office to see what benefits they can get, and tell everyone they know how unfair the whole situation is. These are the stereotypical people you see in the movies heading straight for the local pub to drown their sorrows and share their sob story with anyone who will listen. This will certainly delay them from finding opportunities that may be right in front of them. I feel sorry for whoever is working the bar that day.

When Bill Gates was heralded in the news for being the richest man alive a few years back, there were those who criticized him for being too rich, owning too much, having too much power or influence, and nobody should be allowed to have that much money. What the critics didn't see, because they didn't want to, is that Bill and Melinda also used their money to set up the world's largest private charitable foundation where they donated over $35Billion worth of their Microsoft stock. The Bill & Melinda Gates Foundation is working to improve global health and eradicate polio. If he wasn't rich, none of this could happen.

https://www.forbes.com/profile/bill-gates/#5a5102ec689f

When you become rich, what will you do with your money and what will you want people to say about you? This is a serious question because how you react to others now who are making it rich will have a huge impact on how you become rich and your life as a rich person. Would you congratulate or scorn someone like Bill Gates? He's certainly not perfect, as none of us are, but if he was not rich, he could not be donating the kind of money he does to help others. Oh, I'm not saying there haven't been mistakes and wrong-doings along the way. I'm not saying that the ends always justify the means, either. What I am saying is that if you exist in a world where you have a lack mindset and make a habit of criticizing those who make it to the top, you will find much difficulty in reaching the top yourself. You create abundance when you recognize others for their achievements because something inside you begins to understand that there is enough to go around for everyone and you could have a piece of that someday.

I Luvz Money Exercise: Celebrate

This may be one of the tougher exercises in the book. Look through the media stories of today and try to find a positive story about someone or some company that has recently done something big with lots of money. Maybe it was an acquisition, merger, donation, stocks going up, built a new corporate headquarters, won the lottery, started a new charity, or someone just bought/sold a multi-million dollar mansion. Take a moment in your head or out loud to congratulate them, pray for them, and honestly wish them well in their new adventure. This is paying it forward for when you are there someday. Now, repeat this every time you hear of another story until it becomes a habit to hear this type of news and immediately say to yourself, "Good for them. I wish them the best of luck".

THIS IS ALL A BUNCH OF CRAP!

"What is a belief? It's a feeling of certainty about what something means. Beliefs create the maps that guide us toward our goals and give us the power to take action."

~ Anthony Robbins

Before we can outline a plan of action for becoming rich, the most important thing is that you absolutely must believe it is possible for you to become rich and that you deserve to be. Nothing I do or say after this will help if you don't believe. You have to be able to see it, in full High Definition, for us to proceed and have complete faith in your ability to achieve success. Beyond belief, you will also need an extreme desire to persevere through the inevitable obstacles that will hit you square in the face like a boxer's right cross.

I've been to a whole lot of personal development seminars and I've read a ton of self-help books. Every time I came away saying that the information was decent, but I could tear it apart. The speaker used too many ah's and um's. The other participants were annoying, needy, whiners. This material might work well in the big city where there is more opportunity, but not here in small-town New Hampshire. The presenter never had to go through hard times the way we did. This stuff is all mental garbage with no real action plan. I thought we were going to learn how to change our lives and all they want us to do is cry with a partner all weekend. Why am I walking in circles pretending to be on a beach somewhere? Holy Cow! My partner in this exercise is a real basket case.

This is the kind of head trash that held me back for years. I spent tens of thousands of dollars at seminars only to return home and tear it all apart by finding the faults in it all. It wasn't until decades later that I finally accepted the teachings, found my belief, cast aside my doubts, followed the methods presented, and achieved success. It is so very true that the path to success is by passing through who you once were. For some, this means you need to hit rock bottom to finally accept the truth. For others, like me, it's even worse. It meant years of suffering through an existence of just getting by, wanting more, and pushing it away to remain in my comfort zone.

One of my mentors, Nick Cokinos, was fond of saying, "A crisis is better than a sloppy situation". A crisis is something that needs to be dealt with and requires action. A sloppy situation can linger for years without improving. I was a sloppy situation until I accepted the knowledge that I'm sharing with you and I pray that you get it through your head quicker than I did.

Here are all the mental gymnastics we need to begin with in order for the nuts and bolts to be effective.

BELIEF - first you must absolutely believe that you can become successful in whatever endeavor you choose and whichever road you travel.

MONEY - learn to say "I Luvz Money!" loud and proud and in public. Money is your friend and your tool on the path to wealth. It is not the root of all evil and it wants to help you become who you were meant to be in order to help others do the same.

ABUNDANCE - think constantly in terms of the abundance that surrounds you all the time. Learn to look at everything as a learning experience. Change terms that create judgement, such as good and bad, into phrases that empower you.

OPPORTUNITY - remember that opportunity is all around you, if you are open to it, looking for it, and welcoming it into your life.

CELEBRATE - take time to recognize and celebrate victories small and large. When you do, these victories will come to you more often. When you are truly thinking abundantly, you will also celebrate the failures for the lessons they provide.

CONGRATULATE - celebrate other's successes also. Not just the people you know, but those in the news making headlines for doing something good or accomplishing news-worthy victories. Never be jealous of their success. Congratulate them even if it's quietly to yourself.

PREPARE - there will be losses and failures on the road to success. Prepare for those, not with a lack mindset, but just accepting the eventuality that not everything is going to go as planned.

GRATITUDE - always be on the lookout for ways to express gratitude. Give praise, thanks, and recognition as often as possible. If there is no other person to whom you own some gratitude, then give a prayer of thanks to the One who gives you everything.

If you think this all a bunch of hooey, motivational garbage, or ra-ra-pump-you-up stuff, then I encourage you to give it a try anyway. Without a moment's doubt or hesitation, I can say that not following these mental strategies first, is what caused all my failures in the past. Looking back at all my successes, each and every one was preceded by a firm belief and a positive attitude. If you listen to any of the motivational speakers who have become successful and are now rich, they will tell you it all starts in the head and goes nowhere until the brain is engaged.

Now that we have our heads on straight, we can start getting down to the nitty-gritty.

"We keep moving forward, opening new doors, and doing new things, because we're curious and curiosity keeps leading us down new paths."

~ Walt Disney

I Luvz Money Exercise: It's not crap!

If you have ever read something in personal development and thought it was all a bunch of crap, go back and read it again. Thank the author for sharing their wisdom. Try the exercises. Believe in the process. Begin to accept that those who have become successful before you may know something that you don't.

Is there a local personal development course you can enroll in soon?

Is there a book club you can join?

Is there a Bible study group you can get into?

Part Two Summary

Adopting the Money Mindset without losing your soul.

Like Carl in 'Yes Man', start saying YES! to more opportunities, and like Sir Richard says, "say, yes - then learn to do it later!"

Remember that what's in your head has real power in the real world. *"Watch your thoughts, they become your words; watch your words, they become your actions; watch your actions, they become your habits; watch your habits, they become your character; watch your character, it becomes your destiny."* ~ Lao Tzu, ancient Chinese philosopher

Change your words to reflect an abundance mindset and you will work your way to the top of Maslow's pyramid.

There is no such thing as luck. We make our own fortune.

Think bigger than ever before. Make your plans so crazy big that you will work 10x harder to achieve them.

Make sure your WHY is always bigger than your BUT.

Affirmations are cute, but action plans will eat them for breakfast.

Congratulate those who succeed before you and pay it forward. Celebrate their victories.

Personal development courses are not crap! What's crap is spending all that time and money, then not doing anything with the knowledge. Put it to work and stop being a Doubting Thomas.

PART THREE
WHAT'S THE PLAN?

"Growing your money is a lot like farming. It requires planting, weeding, fertilizing and watering. There is daily work involved in order to reap a rich harvest. This is where most people, arguably 80%, simply don't want to put in the effort to bear more fruit than is necessary for basic survival. They would rather scratch the soil to find a few morsels here and there than plant a field and work it. If you want to become rich, you must get out in the field daily, take care of the crops, store for the winter, and give seeds back to the soil for the next season. When you have more than you need, give some to the farmers next door and teach them to do the same."

~ Matthew Randall

HOW WILL YOU GET RICH?

So, how exactly do you get rich?

Here it is. The part you have all been waiting for. The secret to getting rich. Ready?

Spend less than you make and invest the difference wisely.

That's it. That's the secret sauce. Thanks for reading. Mic drop!

Seriously. That's all there is to it. You can stop here and start planning what you will do with your millions.

What? You want more? OK.

Here's some Madonna for ya,

"Got my diamonds, got my yacht, got a guy I adore.

I'm so happy with what I got, I want more!

Count your blessings, one, two, three

I just hate keeping score.

Any number is fine with me

As long as it's more

As long as it's more!

I'm no mathematician, all I know is addition

I find counting a bore.

Keep the number mounting, your accountant does the counting.

[More! More!]"

~ Madonna, 'More', I'm Breathless album

MATT'S DEFINITION OF RICH

"rich" - adjective

1: having abundant possessions and especially material wealth

2a: having high value or quality

2b: well supplied or endowed

https://www.merriam-webster.com/dictionary/rich

To get started, we need a fresh look at what it means to be rich. In my personal opinion, backed up by a ton of reading that has been done on the subject, I think there are 4 basic levels of wealth and this is how I describe them in simple terms.

Poor - Existing below the poverty level is the standard definition of being poor. If this is the case, then in 2019, the US Government defines poverty as 1 person in the household making less than $12,490 per year and 2 making less than $16,910. The numbers are slightly higher for Alaska and Hawaii, not sure why, don't really care, but that's how the government determines poverty and the applicable social welfare services available to the less fortunate. https://aspe.hhs.gov/poverty-guidelines

My definition is not so clear. I think that poor is not a measure of income, but a state where someone is making less income than they have in basic needs and living expenses. When someone does not make enough to cover their needs at the bottom of Maslow's scale; food, water, clothing, shelter, etc., that is poverty and it can exist at many different income levels. Having said that, if someone is attempting to live beyond their means and well above the level of their income, but they have the means to buy the necessities of survival, then they are not poor because they still have resources and the ability to bring things into budget. I will also contend that poor is more a state of mind than a statement of bank accounts.

Middle-class - When a person has the basics, has enough, wants more, but still needs to show up at work every Monday because their house of cards would all fall apart very quickly if they didn't or couldn't, that's what I call the Middle-class Curse.

"Most people work just hard enough not to get fired and get paid just enough money not to quit."

~ George Carlin

I figure this is just about 80% of our population in the good ol' USofA. We will talk about the 80% Problem later, but for now, think about how many people you know who are maybe a month away from being flat broke if they didn't show up for work tomorrow.

Wealthy - Living with a high income and net worth, all the fun toys, material possessions, leisure time to vacation often, but still living for the paycheck and bound to a job, is what I consider wealthy. These are the people we admire and envy most because they are hard-working, but making more than we are, have more, and do more. We can understand them because they work like we do, but make a whole lot more. Their office is on a higher floor, but they are there every Monday morning, like we are. We want to be there.

"There is a gigantic difference between earning a great deal of money and being rich."

~ Marlene Dietrich

Rich - Are you ready for this? My definition of being rich is not how much money you make, but how your money makes more money for you. When you have reached a point where you no longer need to work a 'J.O.B.' because your money is working for you, that is rich. You are no longer an employee, your money is your employee. When you spend your time managing your money instead of showing up at the office, that is my view of truly rich versus just wealthy. When you go on vacation and you still get a paycheck, that is rich. This is where the term 'passive income' comes into play.

In my family, we grew up with a dream of becoming rich that still resonates with me today and I don't think my parents understood how accurate it was. They certainly didn't understand how to get there. We would often say, "I wish I had enough money to invest that I could just live off the interest." Yup, that's rich in a nutshell and the best part is that almost anyone can make it happen. Yes, even you and me. Unfortunately, my parents thought it only applied to lottery winners.

Being rich does mean all those things that my friends responded with on Facebook; happiness, freedom, never have to work again, do what you want when you want, having enough to give to all my family members, etc. The problem is most of them don't know how to get to that point. Let's take a good look at the two basic ways to make that happen.

I Luvz Money Exercise: Being Rich!

If you had enough money to do "what you want, when you want", what would you do with all that time, money, and energy?

Dream big!

THE TWO ROADS TO RICHES

"If you would be wealthy, think of saving as well as getting."

—Benjamin Franklin

You can become rich by traveling down two roads and often you can travel both at the same time. You can spend less and save wisely, or you can make more and invest wisely. These are the two primary choices. Yes, you can spend less while making more and that will get you there quicker. Many immigrants come to this country and understand the two roads quite well. They live frugally while working hard and making far more than they could in their native country. I have friends who came from other countries and have been become very wealthy by living in cheap apartments, sharing rooms and beds with family members, working 20 hours a day for years to save every penny and invest it for their children. The parents sacrifice their time and energy to give their kids opportunities that they will never have.

ROAD #1: LIVING FRUGALLY

There are many financial experts on TV, radio, and in countless books who will advocate living frugally and living within your means. That works great for those who are on a fixed income or have the mindset that they will never be able to earn more than what they are doing now. Living within your means is a great idea. Cutting expenses is a great idea. Not overspending your budget is a great idea. But...I see two problems (I don't like to use the word problem very often as it represents lack) with this approach. One, cutting expenses may save you from financial ruin and it is smart to limit your expenses, but, two, its no fun and won't make you rich as expenses will always rise with inflation and life will hit you square in the face with unexpected expenses at the worst time.

My wife and I worked hard in a very small business when we were young and dating. We saved to afford the big wedding and a nice honeymoon. The day was beautiful and the cruise to Bermuda was perfect. We planned to wait a few years to have children as we were very busy growing our business and felt that about 3 years would put us in a secure financial position to afford to feed another mouth in the house. When we came back from the honeymoon pregnant, that changed our plans significantly. Oops! I'm not a great dancer. Rhythm is not my strong point and nobody mentioned to us how stress can affect a menstrual cycle. Life has a funny way of changing the best-laid plans of mice and men.

A baby on the way, right out of the gate, and we figured we could handle that. Then, my wife develops gestational diabetes early in the process, our son proves to be a difficult pregnancy and later a challenging birth. In the end, we love him dearly, but he cost us $10,000 in unexpected medical expenses. I kid you not, as I am writing this, (Law of Attraction in action) my wife and son walked in the room and began harassing me again about how I was handing out business cards to the nursing staff during his delivery because we needed a way to pay for the hospital bill. I swear they will write about it on my tombstone someday. And, anyway, what's wrong with drumming up some business between labor pains? I mean it's not like there was anything else to do while we waited for the next contraction. Can we get a little support for those fathers who struggled for nine months, too?

"The habit of saving is itself an education; it fosters every virtue, teaches self-denial, cultivates the sense of order, trains to forethought, and so broadens the mind."

—T.T. Munger

Living frugally may mean cutting back on the things you enjoy. Cutting the cable bill. Making coffee at home instead of going to the drive-thru. Keeping the heat low in the winter. Using a fan instead of AC in the summer. Eating in, not out. Renting movies instead of going to the theatre. Going to the electronics store to watch television. Cutting your own hair. Shopping for clothes at the thrift store and telling your friends you are going through your 'retro chic' stage. The list could go on all day for ways you could save hundreds of dollars a month. The problem I have with this, as an exclusive road to travel, is that it is a very slow and painfully un-fun way to live your life.

There was a television show decades ago called "The Love Boat". It was set on a cruise ship and every week the premise was that people would fall in love on the boat with the help of an amazingly attentive crew. One episode I still remember after all these years was about a retired couple, probably in their 70's, who went on the cruise. The details are a bit fuzzy, but over dinner the husband asks the wife how she could afford to take them on this cruise after so many years of struggling, especially considering that they are now retired and living on a fixed income. He noticed that she had a habit of re-using tea bags. She would use one, wrap it and put it in her purse for later. The wife explained that he would give her a budget for groceries every week and she would be very frugal with her spending, like re-using tea bags. The few dollars she would save from the grocery bill she invested in stocks without him knowing. She further explained that she chose the stocks based on the terms of endearment that her husband would call her. If he called her the 'apple of his eye', she would buy Apple stock and so forth. She then explained that they could afford this cruise because they were now millionaires. The husband was outraged! He said he was so angry because they spent all their good years struggling and now they have money but are too old to enjoy it. The story ends well, by the way, because it's called "The Love Boat" not "The Divorce Boat".

I suppose that story left a lasting impression on me as a child because we went through times where we needed to cut back and live frugally also. I knew, even then, that I didn't want to get to the end of my life and remember it as being nothing more than times of struggle for existence and living beneath my full potential. Here is where I will bring back Wallace Wattles from the very first chapter.

"WHATEVER may be said in praise of poverty, the fact remains that it is not possible to live a really complete or successful life unless one is rich. No man can rise to his greatest possible height in talent or soul development unless he has plenty of money; for to unfold the soul and to develop talent he must have many things to use, and he cannot have these things unless he has money to buy them with."
~ Wallace D. Wattles, 'The Science of Getting Rich'

If this is the only road you plan to travel, then go for it. Live as frugally as you can and invest your savings for the future. Plan for inflation. Work hard and ask for a raise or promotion often. In Part Four, we will talk about a very sound strategy for savings and investment, but for now, make sure you have a savings account and be absolutely disciplined about adding to it regularly. Hopefully, you will do well enough to enjoy retirement comfortably.

For more information on living frugally, I would recommend the book "The Millionaire Next Door", by Thomas J. Stanley Ph.D.,

William D. Danko Ph.D. The works by Dave Ramsey would also be good references.

For those who want a faster road to riches...

ROAD #2: MAKING MORE MONEY

This is where I choose to live. Yes, I watch my budget, but that isn't very fun, if we have to admit it. Controlling every penny. Making sure we don't overspend. Saving for life's little eventualities, like an unexpected child (we love you, kid!). Sounds like too much work to me and it may have to happen for a short period of time your life, but my goal is to work less and earn more. If that sounds like more fun to you, then let's explore options.

First, let me say, that I am not against working for another company. Just because I have been self-employed since I was 17 doesn't mean I am opposed to being an employee. I know it sounds like it to my friends, and for that, I apologize publicly here and now. Indeed, I had my first job at 15 and have worked for other companies over the years, to fill in extra time, make extra income, to learn new skills, and for 4 years teaching high school to keep close tabs on our son who struggled through school. Oh, the sacrifices we make for our kids. I think a person can still become rich while working for someone else, but that is simply not for me.

There are so many ways you can make more money, even while working as an employee. I am a huge fan of creating a side hustle, a sideline, a part-time business, additional income stream. You can purchase investment property. Learn to invest in the stock market. Become a writer, actor, speaker, or presenter of some sort. Internet sales. Be a blogger and monetize your site. At this point, I have done all of these and still have my hands in many.

One of my favorites is network marketing. Yes, I know, for quite a few people that industry turns them off. I believe this is because through the 1970s and 80s, as the industry hit its stride, the marketing approach was simply terrible and it developed a bad reputation. Some companies had disreputable business practices and poor-quality products. Didn't many traditional brick-and-mortar businesses also have their fair share of problems? I think this reputation though was well-earned in its time, but that has changed, and network marketing is now a respectable industry with a solid business model.

Here are some ideas to get the creative juices flowing. Remember to think in turns of endless possibilities and opportunities.

We have a friend, who is an elementary school teacher, who gathers smooth rocks from rivers and the ocean. She paints wonderful and creative designs on them, then sells the rocks online through Etsy, eBay, and other sites. = Active Income, Side Hustle

My sister, that's another story for a biography down the road, just told me a story about her neighbor who had insomnia. He took the time he couldn't sleep and started writing a fiction novel without telling his wife. He sent the book out and found a publisher. One night he took his wife out for a very expensive dinner and told her that he just received a large check for publishing the book she knew nothing about. Now, he's talking with producers about movie or television scripting for the book. = Active Income, Royalties, Future Growth Potential

Have you heard the story about these college students who were playing around with a new website concept to gather pictures of college women and give them a rating system? Yup. That's now

Facebook. = So many streams of income I'm not even sure what to call it

I starred in a local independent film with an attorney who is also an actor and musician. He has written several screenplays in his spare time. A few of these have made it to the national film festivals and it looks like one may be picked up for a major motion picture soon. = Hobby, Potential Income, Royalties, Future Growth Potential

I know a woman who turned her love for making afghans into a full-time sewing and fabric shop. = Active Income

My friend and mentor, Josh, was living in his car with his family and losing his home to foreclosure when he got started in his network marketing business. He is now a millionaire traveling the world and teaching others how to build a business. = Passive Income and Active Income

When my wife and I were just dating back in BC (before children), I received a small inheritance from my grandmother. We used it for the down payment on a four-unit apartment house. We lived in each unit, fixing, repairing, and upgrading as we went along. The rent from the other three units paid the mortgage and expenses so we could live rent-free. Now, we own more rental property, both residential and commercial, that provide us with consistent passive income. If we had chosen to buy a single-family home or another expense that wouldn't create income, we would be where 80% of America is right now...working ourselves into an early grave and living paycheck-to-paycheck, waiting for the day when we can spend our Golden Years relaxing on the porch. = Passive Income

With the exception of getting huge checks from publishing houses or movie producers and making millions on royalties, also called passive income, the smaller side hustles I mentioned may not make you rich on their own. A mentor in the martial arts once told me, "You won't get rich teaching martial arts. You will get rich by what you do with the money you make from teaching martial arts." He was so very right. Whatever road you take remember that it's not how much you make, but what you do with it that will make you rich. Save where you can and invest where you can.

I Luvz Money Exercise: Two Roads

What are some ways you can save money or spend less?

Are there things you spend money on that are not supporting your goal of becoming rich?

What are some ways you can begin to make more money?

Could you start a side hustle?

Could you pick up a weekend job?

Could you turn a hobby into a side business?

Are there additional products or services you could offer?

THE 70-10-10-10 RULE

"This means that if you spend everything you make now, you'll have no choice but to work longer and harder. But if you start investing in your financial future now, you'll have many choices. You can retire early, travel more, continue your career or start a new career later in life. Once again, it all comes down to choices. Think tomorrow today...and live better tomorrow."

~ Jim Rohn, https://www.success.com/rohn-3-keys-to-becoming-wealthy/

The first task to be absolutely consistent with is to set up a new budget called 70-10-10-10. Whether you live on a tight budget or have more gold than Solomon, following a system of budgeting, saving, investing, and giving is critical. The 70% rule or budgeting model is so solid that I'm often shocked by how many people who have never heard of it. Much credit is given today to Jim Rohn for making it more popular and public, but it really extends back thousands of years to the idea of tithing.

THE FIRST 10

To 'tithe' is the old form of the word 'tenth' as it applies to a portion of income or goods and implies that 10% of your income should be given to worthy causes. Originally, this meant the church. There are over 100 references in the Old and New Testaments of the Bible that speak to tithing or giving. Why is this so important? I thought we were talking about getting rich and now you're telling me to give it away? Yes. Tithing is so important that it's the first piece of what we need to do with our money, whether we are rich or not, and it comes right off the top.

Leviticus 27:30 New International Version (NIV)

30 A tithe of everything from the land, whether grain from the soil or fruit from the trees, belongs to the Lord; it is holy to the Lord.

Not that I want to dive deeply into the Bible here, that will be saved for another book, but the first tenth of our income belongs to God, charity, the church, or the community in some fashion. Originally, that was specified as being given to the church. I believe it was important as those who took care of the church made it their full-time profession and had no time for gardening. They needed to eat in order to carry out God's work. The church would then give back to those in the community who needed assistance. Many churches do the same today, but also there are so many other community organizations that need our help and do good work.

An offering is something you give in addition to the tithe. Bill Gates, Warren Buffet and many more have pledged to give over half their earnings to various charities. When you are rich, I hope you will do the same. For now, take 10% off the top and decide where it will be donated. Give cheerfully and generously.

2 Corinthians 9:7 New International Version (NIV)

7 Each of you should give what you have decided in your heart to give, not reluctantly or under compulsion, for God loves a cheerful giver.

THE SECOND 10

After tithing, there is the concept of 'pay yourself first'. Wait! I thought we paid God first? Yes, we did. Now it's your turn. Pay yourself first simply means that you make saving a priority.

before you pay your bills, buy groceries, or do anything else, put away 10% in savings.

There have been many terms for this savings account over the years; savings, emergency fund, fun fund, and "sleep well because I have cash in the bank fund". I prefer that we think of it as an 'opportunity fund'. When an opportunity arises that can advance our goals, there is money set aside to take advantage of that. It's like a 0% interest bank loan and requires no collateral or annoying paperwork.

Let's assume that part of your plan is to invest in rental property. You have some money saved in your opportunity fund and the perfect house comes on the market. Now you have an instant down payment and can take advantage of the opportunity without waiting for the bank. The smart thing to do next would be to replace those funds as soon as possible from the investment so that you are not starting from scratch but rather building from you where you left off.

THE THIRD 10

The third 10% goes into long-term investing for retirement and wealth building. It's still part of 'pay yourself first' and is often referred to as passive investments which may also help to offer some tax sheltering. This category is for things such an IRA, 401(k), SIMPLE, SEP, and other investments that may provide passive rates of return, some security for retirement, and keep some out of the government's hands for as long as possible.

THE REMAINING 70

"I'm struggling to make it now on what I have and you're expecting me to live on just 70% of that!?!?!?!" Yes. Suck it up buttercup, if you want to become rich. Paying yourself first and giving to charity may mean making some personal sacrifices and cutbacks in the short term. Have faith. This formula has been making people rich for over 2000 years.

Keeping this formula in mind, the next step on the road to riches is to make sure you are consistent with your 70-10-10-10 action plan.

Oh, just to be completely open, and to set an example, I promise to tithe 10% of the sales of this book.

I Luvz Money Exercise: 70-10-10-10

I will tithe/donate 10% of my gross earnings to:

I will put 10% of my gross earnings into this savings account:

I will invest 10% of my gross earnings in this type of account:

For a very short period of time, I will need to make these personal sacrifices to live on just 70% of what I am accustomed to:

Take a few deep breaths now and repeat out loud:

I Luvz Money!

I Luvz Money!

I Luvz Money!

I Luvz Money!

I Luvz Money!

I Luvz Money!

I Luvz Money!

I Luvz Money!

It's all going to be OK…

CONSISTENCY IS THE 80% PROBLEM AND SOLUTION

"Forget 'CRYPTO', the fortune is in consistency."

~ George Campbell & Jim Packard, Consistency is the New Currency

By now, almost everyone has heard of Vilfredo Pareto and the 'Pareto Principle' or the '80/20 Rule'. In relation to the subject of this book, 80% of your wealth will come from 20% of your efforts, and so forth. I first heard this so many years ago that I can't even remember when and it has been used to describe everything possible. In sales, 80% of your income will come from the top 20% of your customers. 80% of your sales will come from 20% of your sales team. At work, 80% of the work will be done by the top 20% of your employees. In my martial arts business, those who made it big would often say that your instructors can only hope to be 80% as good as you are at teaching. This can be used in almost every situation and would most likely be accurate.

I owe a huge debt of gratitude to Jim Packard, co-author of 'Consistency is the New Currency' for giving me a copy of his book. It finally explained why it took so long for me to sit down and write 'I Luvz Money'. You see, I am what they call an '80%-er'. The reason why it took me so long to make some serious money is that I'm an '80%-er'. The reason for why I had fits and starts with my business and therefore my bank accounts for so many years, was because I am an '80%-er'. Chances are you might be an '80%-er' as well.

What does it mean to be an '80%-er'? I would highly recommend you read the book, but to give it an oversimplified review, 80% of the population isn't rich because we haven't been consistent enough with our plans and actions. Consistency is the missing ingredient. Lack of consistency leads to self-sabotage and a roller coaster of ups and downs with our jobs, businesses, relationships, and money. The book explains it much better, but that's the executive summary. This book finally explained why I've been so inconsistent, that it's OK and normal for 80% of the population, it's not a lack of education or talent, it's a really a root software issue. Like so many others, I was born to sprint, not marathon when it comes to getting things done or achieving goals. I do well in short bursts of energy that produce short-term results. Long-term goals are very tough for me and I lose focus easily. This has been shown to be common for about 80% of the population and it's a major reason why we aren't rich.

What can be done about this for us '80%-ers'? Jim and George will tell you that it takes one simple action every day, consistently, and they have a terrifically simple phone app to help. For me, in writing this book, I made it a goal to spend one hour each day free writing my thoughts and experiences. To become rich can be just as simple. If you are not yet, then you might also be an '80%-er'. Together we can make a plan and be successful, as long as you are willing to take one simple action every day towards achieving your goal.

Ideas for daily actions may be:

- making one more phone call
- writing a short blog post
- one hour writing in your book
- journaling
- posting a video to your website
- Facebook live video

- emailing one customer
- recognizing an employee
- asking for a referral
- sending a personal note to a customer
- read 10 pages a day on personal development

I'm sure you can come up with more, and I'll ask you to in the exercise for this chapter. The point is that it doesn't have to be earth-shattering. It just needs to be consistent and daily. As simple as it seems, this process and commitment to yourself can have profound effects on your success, your income, and your self-esteem. Don't overcomplicate it. Just pick one simple action to add to your day.

Are you ready to get started?

Are you ready to take on one simple daily task and be consistent with it?

I Luvz Money Exercise: One Simple Daily Action

What is one simple action towards your goal that you can take, every day, to remind you how easy it is to create consistency in your life and build a healthy habit?

YOUR PERSONAL MIRACLE MORNING

"Considering that our habits create our life, there is arguably no single skill that is more important for you to learn and master than controlling your habits. You must identify, implement, and maintain the habits necessary for creating the results you want in your life, while learning how to let go of any negative habits which are holding you back from achieving your true potential."

~ Hal Elrod, 'The Miracle Morning'

Here is where, for the sake of getting right to the point, I will give a quick summary of Hal Elrod's books beginning with 'The Miracle Morning'. I feel these Miracle Mornings are so critical to your success that they deserve a chapter. I can tell you that creating my miracle morning has made a huge difference in my success as well as my mental health. I wake up energized and excited to begin the day, yes…even on Monday mornings.

In his books, he describes interviewing the most successful people in the world and discovered that they all have a morning routine that includes very similar elements. Elrod believes this miracle morning routine is a major factor in their success and I agree. Hopefully, this will encourage you to read his books and adopt your own personal miracle morning success routine. If this is what the rich and famous do, then wouldn't it be worth a try to model that behavior?

It all begins with having a good night's sleep. In my opinion, nothing helps me to sleep better than knowing that all the bills will be paid. Money worries and money stress will kill a good sleep and ruin your health, so it is very important that we work towards learning to Luvz Money and becoming rich as soon as possible.

Here is what Elrod recommends for a daily ritual.

First, Elrod recommends you always have a large glass of water immediately upon waking.

After your morning personal needs; potty time, teeth brushing, etc., start your miracle morning and allow no more than 1 hour for the entire routine of 6 parts.

Silence - Prayer, meditation, moment of silence, reflection

Affirmations - Positive self-talk, mantras, and action plan

Visualization - See the success you desire

Exercise - Morning is the best time, you can do more later, just get your body moving

Reading - You are what you read, find your inspiration, 10 pages

Scribing - Writing, planning, journaling, idea generation

The order in which you do all six parts isn't as important as making sure you get them all completed within an hour. Generally speaking, starting with silence is the best place. If that produces some ideas that should be written down then maybe scribing could come next. Exercise could come last on some days. It's all good. Just make it happen and enjoy the process. Possibly the first reading you do should be 'The Miracle Morning' to lay the foundation? Just a thought.

Since beginning to use a Miracle Morning routine of my own, I have noticed better focus and energy throughout the day. Something else that helps is to write down your goals for the next day just before bed. This takes a load off your mind and helps to promote more restful sleep.

I Luvz Money Exercise: My Miracle Morning

Write down your personal plan for a miracle morning.

60 MINUTES: What time will you get up to start?

SILENCE: What will be your meditation or prayer focus today?

AFFIRMATION: Remember in a previous chapter we discussed how traditional affirmations don't really work? Let's change the term here to ACTION MANTRAS:

VISUALIZATION: See you as a success in full living color. What is something you truly want to succeed in?

EXERCISE: What form of exercise will you start with?

READING: What will you begin reading?

SCRIBING: Do you have a journal or notebook of some kind to begin writing your thoughts, goals, dreams, and ideas?

USING THE 5 W'S TO MAKE SMART MONEY DECISIONS

"Nearly one-third of lottery winners eventually declare bankruptcy."

~Consumer Financial Protection Bureau

Let's play with this dream for a moment. If you are making, just for example, $32,000 (yay, 1%-ers of the World!) and I were to hand you a winning lottery ticket for 10 million dollars right now, what would you do with it? The immediate response from most people is, "I would quit my job, buy a huge house and a car, maybe a few cars, and pay off bills, of course, and put money away for the kid's college, and go on a vacation around the world…"

A winning lottery ticket would be amazing and there is certainly so much fun that could be had with that kind of play money, but I would humbly suggest, the first thing to do with all that cheddar would be to consult a trusted financial advisor and an attorney. Not Uncle Ralph! Someone not in your family who doesn't stand to inherit anything. Please.

Back on track again, unless you have a carefully crafted bucket list of what you will do when you become rich and what that means to you, the unfortunate truth is that it will probably never happen. You'll wake up one morning and wonder where all the time went so quickly and you have nothing to show for it. Sad, yes, but that's what happens to about 80% of the population and it is often called a 'mid-life crisis'. Mid-life is that time in the 40s when people wake up to the reality that they are getting to a point where half of their good years are gone and they didn't achieve most of the items on their bucket list from when they were young and healthy enough to do them. This includes taking the opportunities presented and making the money they feel they should have. I'm hoping this book serves as a kick in the pants to prevent that from happening to you and a roadmap to success.

I've been through SMART goals, vision boards, seminars, gurus, mentors, coaches, and such an incredible array of self-help books that are now 'shelf-help' books. I'm not saying that they haven't been worth the time and money, because they have. Everything we read and experience combines to lead us where we are today and who we are today. We are the total of our experiences, and yet, sometimes we are still not where we feel we should be. Why is that? The answer may simply be, we feel this way because we haven't completed the tasks we set out to achieve.

Most of the time we are not where we want to be financially or feel we deserve to be only because…(ready for some more harsh reality)…we simply don't always make smart decisions with our money. Sorry. That's the truth and I have been a victim of this also. I have learned to use a formula called 'The 5 W's' to help make solid financial decisions and prevent irrational decisions. This tends to keep me more consistent in following through with action steps because I believe my choices are based on careful planning and sound reasoning.

The 5 W's is a simple formula I use for making decisions about money matters. This would include spending, making, saving, investing, donating, and all other money decisions.

1. WHY - always begin with why. Why do I want to do this with my money? Why do I really want to buy this? Why do I want to invest in this particular project or charity?

2. WHO - who will be affected by this decision? As a member of Rotary International, we open each weekly meeting with the following questions which provide some good guidance in many situations, including money matters:

    Is it the truth?

    Is it fair to all concerned?

    Will it build goodwill and better friendships?

    Will it be beneficial to all concerned?

3. WHERE - where will the money go or where will it come from? A good friend of mine uses the question, "Who is going to pay for this?" What he means by this is really where will the money come from? He expects that it will be from an outside source, a new sale, a gift, a new opportunity, or anything other than directly from himself. If he is going to purchase something, he makes a habit of finding some new creative way to pay for it rather than from his own bank account. Not always easy to do, but a good policy to work with.

4. WHEN - do I need to do this right now, or can it wait? Prevents impulse buys and rash decisions?

5. WHAT - what will be the consequence of this decision? Could there be unintentional consequences I haven't considered? What are the long-range ramifications?

The 5 W's are an easy way to keep spending under control and in line with your financial goals. I would recommend going through all of these questions anytime you need to make a major money decision. Maybe it's not necessary when buying a stick of gum or a sub for lunch, but a large screen TV or a new car, probably.

I Luvz Money Exercise: The 5 W's

Let's practice this formula.

What is something you have been wanting to purchase?

Now, ask the questions in this order:

WHY:

WHO:

WHERE:

WHEN:

WHAT:

Part Three Summary

How to get RICH in two easy steps

Spend less, make more.

There is a difference between being wealthy and being rich.

Are there places you can save right now and ways to can learn to earn more later?

Tithe, save, invest, and live within your means. Just make sure your 'means' are always improving.

One simple action daily that you can be consistent with is the key to getting started.

Create your personal miracle morning and enjoy the process.

Keep in mind the 5 W's when making any decision, especially a money decision.

PART FOUR
YOUR LEGACY

"Using our wealth while we are alive to enrich our lives, expand our experiences, and entertain ourselves, may be fun, but it is very selfish and self-serving. Creating a legacy that will live on after you are gone and enrich the lives of others, is a far more noble and worthy endeavor."

~ Matthew Randall

WHAT WILL YOU LEAVE BEHIND?

The Tombstone of Edward George Lytton (1803-1873)

Laborious and distinguished in all fields of intellectual activity

indefatigable and ardent in the cultivation and love of letters

his genius as an author was displayed in the most varied forms

which have connected indissolubly

with every department of the literature of his time

the name of Edward Bulwer-Lytton.

A popular, although macabre, project in some high school classes is the ask the question, "What will be written on your tombstone as an epitaph?" It asks the students to summarize their most important life achievements in one sentence or to commemorate a favorite saying they would be known for. For me, I think my family would choose something like, "I just need to finish this one last…(aaarrrrrr)"

It may seem a bit odd if you are young, but a big part of your WHY needs to include a good look at what you will leave behind. What will happen with all of your money? Will you leave a lasting memory? Who's lives will be affected long after you pass?

For this reason, most of the rich set up trust accounts, foundations, or memorials of some sort to give their lives meaning long after they are dead. The Bill and Melinda Gates Foundation, for instance, will be well-funded long past their expirations. I have sat on the boards of several charitable causes that have permanent funding because someone wealthy left a huge donation that has been invested and will provide interest income for life, if it is maintained properly. Many college scholarships are created in the name of a loved one and provide donations each year to worthy candidates.

Here area few ideas from wealthy celebrities who will be remembered for their generous efforts and contributions:

- Jackie Chan donates his money to build schools in rural China.

- Chuck Norris created a foundation to help inner-city kids get into martial arts training and stay off drugs.

- Ashton Kutcher spends his time and money rescuing children from sexual slavery.

- The Leonard DiCaprio Foundation is devoted to protecting the world's oceans, wildlife, and forests.

- Matt Damon's foundation is dedicated to providing clean water to millions.

- Bette Midler's foundation is more local. The goal is to create green spaces around New York City such as gardens, parks and planting trees.

- Hugh Jackman's foundation provides education and entrepreneurial opportunities in needy communities.

- Emma Watson's foundation works with the United Nations to promote women's rights globally.

Your goals do not need to be global. I know many local rich individuals who have built a new public building, or created a park, donated their home as a homeless shelter, funded a few years of a local drug and alcohol recovery program, donated funds to build a new animal shelter, and one who created a program in locals schools to teach chess to students because his son was a victim of drug abuse and he loved chess.

Other options would be a little more standard. Donating to large research organizations can be a big boost in solving some medical issues. Breast cancer, heart disease, amputations and robotics, vision and hearing loss. These and many more are great causes. I recently discovered that my birth mother died of leukemia at a very early age. That could prompt me to leave some of my estate to a cancer charity or something along that theme.

Why wouldn't I leave it all to my family? You can certainly do that. Whatever your decision is, consult with a qualified estate attorney and financial advisor. Here is my personal opinion. If you have done a good job of setting an example for your children and provided them with a good financial education, then they shouldn't need anything more than burial and other final expenses. They should be on track to make their own money. Now, if they are too young, a trust account would be helpful to ensure they make it through college in sound financial condition with few worries about tuition bills.

Many of the richest individuals in the world plan to leave very little to their children with the understanding that they should make their own money in the world. Will they give them a cushion and some assistance? Yes, but they are wary of the consequences of giving their children tons of money with no restrictions, obligations, or responsibility. This has often led to poor results.

"Most of the (Warren) Buffett estate is already earmarked for charity. The famous investor plans to donate at least $37 billion to the Bill and Melinda Gates Foundation for the advancement of health and educational causes around the world. Buffett has left considerably less for his children, reflecting his expressed interest in promoting self-sufficiency and strong work ethics among his family. The bequests to them include a small amount of Berkshire Hathaway stock and some real estate properties."

~ *https://www.investopedia.com/ask/answers/021615/who-does-warren-buffett-plan-bequeath-his-estate.asp*

What happens if you decide not to decide, not to have a will, and not to have a trust? In April of 2016, the singer Prince passed away unexpectedly. He left behind an estate of almost $200million. He had no plan for his estate, not even a simple will listing his intentions. Forget about a foundation, trust, or other memorial. A man who was surrounded by lawyers and managers never took the time to write a simple one page will. As a result, 2 years later his family hadn't received a penny, but the lawyers raked in over $6million and requested another $3million in fees and expenses.

https://www.forbes.com/sites/markeghrari/2018/04/18/two-years-later-princes-heirs-have-still-not-received-a-penny-of-his-estate/#3ab5a4e43ab2

Unfortunately, this is not unusual for celebrities. In my opinion, it is shameful to let all that hard-earned money go to lawyers instead of family or worthy causes. Others in this list would include Aretha Franklin, Bob Marley, Amy Winehouse, Jimi Hendrix, Sonny Bono, and Kurt Cobain. It was thought that

Michael Jackson died without a will, but his mom found one that was hidden somewhere, just in time.

This list is not limited to celebrities, either. Abraham Lincoln and Dr. Martin Luther King Jr. left the earth unexpectedly without wills. I'm sure that many of these people died so young that they thought they were too young to contemplate their own end and had plenty of time. It is never too early to plan for the end, especially when there are millions of dollars at stake or families who need to survive on your estate.

None of us are getting out of here alive and not all spouses or children are ready to take over the family business or create their own to survive. Mrs. Lincoln and her two sons waited two years to split the $110,300 inheritance 3 ways after Abe's assassination. There was no pension for US Presidents at that time. Dr. King's family has been fighting over control of the estate since 1968. His children are still arguing about whether to sell his Noble Peace Prize medal and personal bible. Sonny Bono was relatively young and healthy at 62. He never expected to die in a skiing accident. His $2million estate was fought over by his wife Mary, ex-wife Cher, and his secret love-child Sean. What a mess.

If you Luvz Money, Luvz your family, Luvz your community, and Luvz your world, then do something good with your riches. Plan for the future and plan for those unexpected unfortunate events that could leave your family fighting with attorneys and courts for years. Previously I mentioned my father and his paranoia about people handling his finances (Luvz you, Dad!). He didn't have a huge estate, but because his will and trust left out a few important items that he had simply forgotten about, his estate had to go to probate court which held up transferring titles, deeds, and business interests for over a year. In the process, some of his estate needed to be used to pay attorneys to straighten it out. It was very frustrating and wasteful. Just get it done so that your wishes and desires for your estate can be taken care of properly. There is plenty of other work for lawyers to do. They don't need your money.

I Luvz Money Exercise: Legacy

What is something you are very passionate about that you could leave a sizable donation to when you are gone?

Is there a foundation you could establish and fund while you are still alive so that you could be on the board and give it your personal direction?

What would you leave to your family if you were rich?

EPILOGUE

/ˈepəˌlôg,ˈepəˌläg/

noun: **epilogue**; plural noun: **epilogues**; noun: **epilog**; plural noun: **epilogs**

1. a section or speech at the end of a book or play that serves as a comment on or a conclusion to what has happened."the meaning of the book's title is revealed in the epilogue"

WHAT ARE YOU READING?

"You are what you read."

~ Oscar Wilde

*"Not all **readers** are **leaders**, but all **leaders are readers**."*

~ Harry S. Truman

There are many books referenced in 'I Luvz Money'. I would encourage you to read them all and continue reading books on personal development as well as money management. Whether you prefer traditional paperbound books, digital format, or audio, always be reading something that will keep you focussed.

Why would I spend time at the end of a book to tell you to keep reading?

Here are some realities that must be dealt with.

I remember a very moving story in one of Anthony Robbins' books or audiotapes. (Apologies to Mr. Robbins and the readers here that I can't find the reference and will most likely badly paraphrase it. Sir, please call me anytime and let me know if I recall this properly. I'll update it in the next version.) It was a particular story he told about when he started to make lots of money. He described how, as he got richer, some of his friends did not. They kept their jobs or businesses and continued to do OK but he outgrew them financially. There was a time when he invited some friends to go for a trip on his private jet. They politely declined. When this happened time after time, he realized that they were uncomfortable with the difference in their socioeconomic status and simply stopped being friends over time because they couldn't compete, keep up, or contribute.

How does this relate to you and me? Well, in order to grow, there are times when you need to leave the past behind. Some of that past will include friends or family who try to keep you where you are so that you don't outgrow them. They will do subtle things to hold you back because they won't be able or won't choose to keep up. Even other business associates may stop associating with you because they can't compete. This has been true in my life and it hurts for a while. Luvz them. Pray for them. Wish them the best. Keep them on your Christmas card list. Call them on their birthday. But! Never let them hold you back from reaching your dreams, even if that means you have to let them go.

In these times of growth and transition (notice I successfully avoided the word 'change' again?), books will become your best friends. They never change. They don't ghost you. They always encourage you to become the best you can be. They lend courage and confidence when friends and family may let you down. They will travel with you on any crazy journey you choose. Books will keep you motivated, educated, focused, and positive as you become the person you were meant to be.

People are not so reliable. You may find that as your economic status improves you will need to let go of those who don't follow you. You may need to change mentors. You may need to move in different social circles. You may find that comments people once made are no longer tolerable as they conflict with your goals. All of this is good and necessary. It does not need to change who you are as a person or alter your character. It may simply be necessary to seek out and hang out with people who will support and encourage you better. Quite often that means associating with people who will lift you up, not hold you down.

I'll be honest with you. There are friends in my life who complain about their jobs all the time. I choose not to hang around that attitude very often as it will infect me and hold me back. There are family members who I don't call any longer because their behavior is negative. There are people who criticize my decision because they fail to understand them. There are business groups that I have outgrown and will not attend those meetings any longer. Please don't mistake this for me being a snob. The word 'decide', coming from the Latin, means to 'cut away or cut off'. We all have decisions to make about who we choose to have in our close circles and they don't need to be personal attacks. We just need to choose wisely who we will associate with as we grow and cut away that which doesn't serve us well. Books will become some of your best friends.

I have found the easiest way to choose which books to read next are to look for the references that influenced authors I respect. All good motivational authors and speakers were influenced by other authors and they give them proper reference whenever possible. Follow the thread to find good reads. Ask your mentors who they read. Ask people who are more successful than you who they read. If you read at least one book every month, that would be more than the average American. To be a power reader and leader, it's one every week.

"Adults with annual household incomes of $30,000 or less are about three times as likely as the most affluent adults to be non-book readers (36% vs. 13%)."

~ *https://www.pewresearch.org/fact-tank/2018/03/23/who-doesnt-read-books-in-america/*

"Most CEOs and executives read 4-5 books per month. These are the leaders, the game changers, the ones that end up shaking the ground, rebuilding industries, providing jobs, and inventing some of our most beloved everyday products. If they're reading that much, then clearly there is still some value in picking up a book."

~ *https://www.inc.com/brian-d-evans/most-ceos-read-a-book-a-week-this-is-how-you-can-too-according-to-this-renowned-.html*

Thank you so much for choosing to read this book. I am eternally grateful and hope that it has provided you with some good information, direction, motivation, and inspiration. Please share it with someone you would like to have with you on your journey to becoming rich. The journey is more fun with friends who share your goals and provide you with some fun competition along the way.

Keep reading and keep growing.

SUGGESTED READING LIST

Many authors give you a list of books to read as back-up or follow-up.

Why? Because the list of books is what inspired them.

I will, instead, give a list of my favorite authors who inspired me and encourage you to read anything and everything by them, in no particular order.

It is with the deepest gratitude and respect that I present:

George Campbell & Jim Packard	Jack Canfield
Robert Kiyosaki	Tim Ferris
Anthony Robbins	Simon Sinek
Norman Vincent Peale	Darren Hardy
Dale Carnegie	Hal Elrod
Napoleon Hill	Noah St. John
Coach John Wooden	David Campbell
Ivan Misner	Jonah Berger
Zig Zigler	Grant Cardone
Dave Ramsey	Dorothy Leeds
Rhonda Byrne	Richard Fenton
Jen Sincero	Tommy Watt
Jordan Adler	Stephen Covey
Les Brown	Ken Blanchard
Wallace D. Wattles	Malcolm Gladwell
Og Mandino	Paulo Coelho
James Allen	Michael Gerber
David Chilton	Harry Palmer
Carol Dweck	

These are just a few of my favorites.
In addition, I love to dive into the much older classics such as:

The Holy Bible	**Plato**
Sun Tzu	**Aristotle**
Lao Tsu	**Socrates**

Just so you don't think I'm all business and no fun, science fiction is my favorite distraction. If you haven't read the 'Dune' series yet, by Frank Herbert, it nearly ruined an entire year of college and almost got me kicked out. Couldn't put it down. I still consider it the standard by which all sci-fi is judged. Just another one of my famous (or infamous) opinions.

One final note from the author...

Thank you so much for investing your time, money, and energy by purchasing this book. I hope it is only one in a long line of books, seminars, workshops, coaching, and other personal development resources that you will invest in. Become a life-long learner and the rewards will be far beyond money. Put these ideas and others you learn into action and believe in yourself. Don't let this book go from 'self-help' to 'shelf-help' where it collects dust. Re-read it and recommend it to friends. Growing personally and financially is always more fun when your friends are along for the ride.

M Randall

With deepest gratitude,

ABOUT THE AUTHOR

Matthew Randall - International man of mystery, jet-setting globe trotter, and savior of the down-trodden.

While that might look like fun on my tombstone, the truth is not quite so illustrious. Really, I'm just an average guy born and raised in a small town of about 4000 that sits on the border between New Hampshire and Maine an hour north of Boston. I went to a very small grade school where there was one class of about 20 kids for each of 6 grades. I think I was number 40 in a graduating class of 140-ish in high school. I commuted a whole 10 miles in college to attend the University of New Hampshire and received a B.A. in Political Science. And, by the way, I truly don't enjoy writing about me, but here it goes...

My father was born and raised in this quaint small town as well, while my mother was an immigrant from Germany. They met while he was in the army, married in Munich, and moved back to New Hampshire to spend the rest of their lives in a small town working in a small family business. My father was a pharmacist, like his father before him, and like I was expected to be next. The family pharmacy had between 6-12 employees at any given time. Not exactly positioned to take over the world and become a conglomerate. This is why we were eventually consumed by big business moving into town.

I was not interested in becoming a pharmacist, so I opened a martial arts school right out of college. What else should one do with a Poli-Sci degree? My interests, however, were not limited to just kicking people in the head every night. Nope. I had much grander ambitions. Sometime, I'll enthrall you with the complete autobiography, but for now, let's say that my interests are wide and varied.

Some of my crazy history would include: I've written three full-length books at this point and several very small personal development manuals. I've been a runway model, an actor, starred in two full-length independent films, and internal training videos for a small company called Liberty Mutual. I'm a business coach, public speaker, real estate investor, property manager, and serial entrepreneur. At this time, I've started 12 businesses. Oh, and I was a world champion competitor three times. If that doesn't just scream ADD, then I'm not sure what does.

Today I live in the same old family farm with my wife of 25+ years (really question her sanity) and our six children (God love them!), one dog, two cats, and way too much lawn to mow.

Does that sound impressive? Don't let it fool you. It just demonstrates the depth of my ADD and all that resume' stuffing won't buy a cup of coffee. While I have been able to perform at high levels for short periods of time in specific endeavors, the ability to maintain that focus long-term has been something I always struggled with and still do to a point. I learned to tame the beast and overcome these challenges. You can, too. That leads to the reason for this book.

I hope to prove a point in this book that you can be a small town kid and still do well. On the same token, you can be a world champion and still not be rich. It's all in your mindset, planning, and desire. You can be whatever you want to be. With this book, I hope to convince you that is a good, noble, honorable, and completely possible for you to become rich, if you want it bad enough. I'm hoping you learn to say, "I Luvz Money!" loud and proud because you earned the right to say it. Will you join me on this journey?